ALSO BY PHILIPPE SANDS

BOOKS

The Ratline
East West Street
City of Lions (with Josef Wittlin)
The Grey Zone (ed.)
Torture Team
Lawless World
Principles of International Environmental Law
Justice for Crimes Against Humanity (ed.)
From Nuremberg to The Hague (ed.)
Bowett's Law of International Institutions

FILM

My Nazi Legacy

PODCAST/RADIO

The Ratline
La Filière

PERFORMANCE

East West Street: A Song of Good and Evil
The Last Colony

The Last Colony

The Last Colony

A Tale of Exile, Justice, and Courage

PHILIPPE SANDS

ALFRED A. KNOPF   New York
2023

Grateful acknowledgment is made to the following for permission
to reprint previously published material:
Extract from *Silence of the Chagos* by Shenaz Patel (Restless Books, 2019).
Reprinted with kind permission of Restless Books, New York. Extract from
"Witness" by Eavan Boland (Carcanet, 1998). Reprinted with kind permission of Carcanet
Press, Manchester, UK. Extract from *Discours sur le colonialisme* (Présence Africaine
Editions, 1955) / Discourse on Colonialism (Monthly Review Press, trans. 2000)
by Aimé Césaire. Reprinted with kind permission of Présence Africaine Editions,
Paris, and Monthly Review Press, New York.

Library of Congress Cataloging-in-Publication Data
Name: Sands, Philippe, [date] author.
Title: The last colony : a tale of exile, justice, and courage / Philippe Sands.
Description: First American edition. | New York: Alfred A. Knopf, 2023. |
"This is a Borzoi book published by Alfred A. Knopf"—title page verso. |
includes bibliographical references and index.
Identifiers: LCCN 2023002837 (print) | LCCN 2023002838 (ebook) |
ISBN 9780593535097 (hardcover) | ISBN 9780593535103 (ebook)
Subjects: LCSH: Population transfers—Chagossians. | Deportation—British Indian
Ocean Territory. | Chagossians—History. | Chagossians—Biography. | Deportees—
British Indian Ocean Territory. | Deportees—Mauritius. | Deportees—Seychelles. |
British Indian Ocean Territory—History—20th century. | British Indian Ocean
Territory—Colonization. | Great Britain—Colonies—Africa—History—20th century.
Classification: LCC DS349.9.C42 S26 2023 (print) | LCC DS349.9.C42 (ebook) |
DDC 969.7—dc23/eng/20230124
LC record available at https://lccn.loc.gov/2023002837
LC ebook record available at https://lccn.loc.gov/2023002838

Jacket photograph: *Rita Élysée Bancoult stands by the sea at Port Louis, Mauritius.*
The Asahi Shimbun / Getty Images. Used by permission of Olivier Bancoult;
(stamp) Pictures from History / Getty Images.
Jacket design by Jenny Carrow

Manufactured in the United States of America
First American Edition

Dedicated to the memory of

James Crawford (1948–2021)

and

Louise Rands Silva (1964–2021)

What is a colony
if not the brutal truth
that when we speak
the graves open.
And the dead walk?

—EAVAN BOLAND, "Witness," 1998

Contents

Note to the Reader

This is a true story, first recounted in a series of lectures I gave at the Hague Academy of International Law in the summer of 2022. As a participant in parts of it, I am not an independent observer, and understand that events may be seen from different angles, with different interpretations. I have tried to present a personal account in a manner that is fair and balanced.

The story, which is little known and deserves a broader audience, actually comprises a number of interwoven tales. One relates to the International Court of Justice in The Hague, and its role in the gradual demise of colonialism, with a focus ultimately on the case of Mauritius. Another is more personal: my own evolving relationship with the world of international law. And a third, the beating heart of this book, is the tale of Liseby Elysé—the wrongs done to her and other Chagossians, and their quest for justice, which continues to this day.

I have sought to capture what Madame Elysé shared with me, during many hours spent together going over the text and the events, to accord with her recollections. I hope that our collaboration and friendship meet her aspirations. Our backgrounds are different, yet our paths connected, through processes of law and litigation that have gradually closed the curtain on the colonial era into which Madame Elysé was born and lived, and in which my working life has been cast.

London and Bonnieux
July 2022

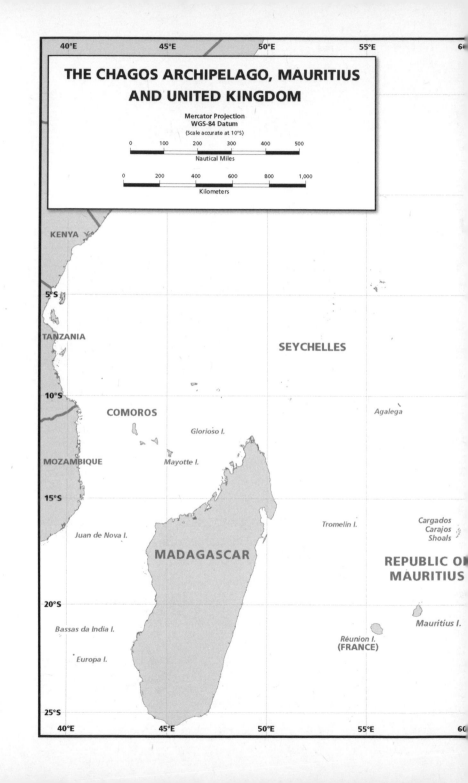

THE CHAGOS ARCHIPELAGO, MAURITIUS
AND UNITED KINGDOM

Mercator Projection
WGS-84 Datum
(Scale accurate at 10°S)

Nautical Miles

Kilometers

KENYA

TANZANIA

SEYCHELLES

COMOROS

Agalega

Glorioso I.

MOZAMBIQUE

Mayotte I.

Tromelin I.

Cargados
Carajos
Shoals

Juan de Nova I.

MADAGASCAR

REPUBLIC OF
MAURITIUS

Mauritius I.

Bassas da India I.

Réunion I.
(FRANCE)

Europa I.

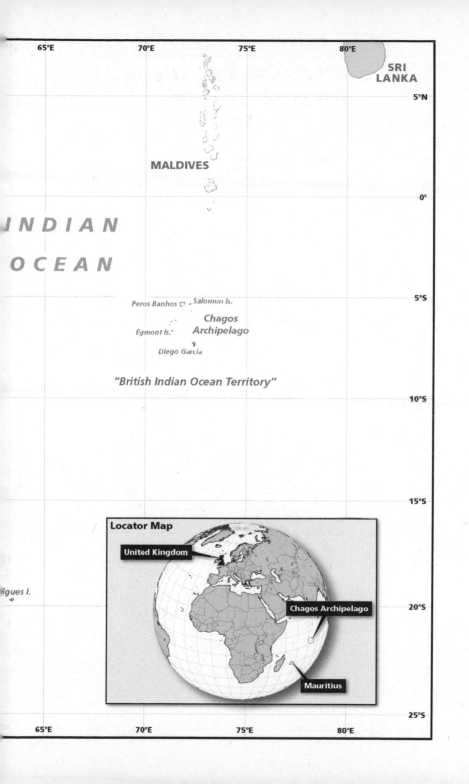

65°E   70°E   75°E   80°E

SRI
LANKA

5°N

MALDIVES

0°

INDIAN

OCEAN

Peros Banhos ☐ . *Salomon Is.*

5°S

*Chagos
Archipelago*

Egmont Is.

Diego Garcia

"British Indian Ocean Territory"

10°S

15°S

Locator Map

United Kingdom

igues I.

Chagos Archipelago   20°S

Mauritius

25°S

65°E   70°E   75°E   80°E

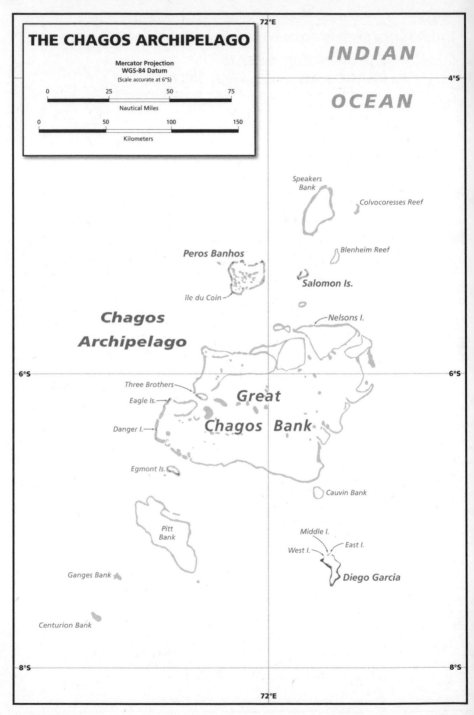

THE CHAGOS ARCHIPELAGO

Mercator Projection
WGS-84 Datum
(Scale accurate at 6°S)

0   25   50   75

Nautical Miles

0   50   100   150

Kilometers

72°E

INDIAN

4°S

OCEAN

Speakers Bank

Colvocoresses Reef

Peros Banhos

Blenheim Reef

Salomon Is.

île du Coin

Chagos
Archipelago

Nelsons I.

6°S

6°S

Three Brothers

Eagle Is.

Great

Danger I.

Chagos Bank

Egmont Is.

Cauvin Bank

Pitt
Bank

Middle I.

West I.

East I.

Ganges Bank

Diego Garcia

Centurion Bank

8°S

8°S

72°E

Plate 2

ANNOTATED EXCERPT FROM BRITISH ADMIRALTY CHART 3

INDIAN OCEAN
CHAGOS ARCHIPELAGO: 1837

Île du Coin

Plate 3

Prologue: "La Cour!"

The Chagos. An archipelago with a name silken as a caress,
fervid as regret, brutal as death . . .

—SHENAZ PATEL, *Silence of the Chagos*, 2005

L a Cour!" On a summer morning in The Hague, the words were proclaimed with solemnity by a man in formal attire from whose neck hung an impressive silver chain, a symbol of authority. As practised for many decades, he announced the languid entry into the Great Hall of Justice of the judges, robed and beribboned, making their way to their respective seats in a line behind a very long table. The President, a calm man from Somalia who knew first-hand what it meant to be on the receiving end of British and Italian colonial generosity, stood at their centre. He glanced around the courtroom, looked at the assembled rows of lawyers and diplomats, journalists and interpreters, framed by vast stained-glass windows and crystal chandeliers, then invited us to take our seats.

Sitting in the second row, directly behind me, was a diminutive lady dressed in black, the small handbag she clutched offering an air of formality, of dignity. She had travelled from distant Mauritius as a member of that country's delegation. She was here to tell a story, a short tale of the early years of her life, in the hope that her account might encourage the fourteen judges in a direction that could allow her to return to the place of her birth. Home, in a real sense, where the heart is, was Peros Banhos, a tiny island that is part of an archipelago called Chagos, located in the midst of a vast Indian Ocean. From there, five decades earlier, along with hundreds of others, she had been forcibly removed.

Liseby Elysé lived happily on Peros Banhos until her twentieth year. Then, without warning, one spring day she was rounded up by the British authorities, allowed a single suitcase, and ordered to board a boat that would transport her a thousand miles away. "The island is being closed," she was told. No one explained why. No one mentioned a new military base the British had allowed the Americans to build on another island, Diego Garcia. No one told her that Chagos, long a part of Mauritius, had been severed from that territory and was now a new colony in Africa, known as the "British Indian Ocean Territory." Madame Elysé, and the entire community of some 1,500 people, almost all Black and many descended from enslaved plantation workers, were forcibly removed from their homes and deported.

She was in The Hague to participate in a case about her islands. The fourteen judges did not yet know who she was, or her role in the proceedings. They would hear arguments about Britain's last colony in Africa, how it was dismembered from Mauritius, and determine whether, as a matter of international law, it belonged to Mauritius or Britain. The judges would navigate matters of history and colonial rule, traversing questions of race and rights under international law. They would confront the principle of "self-determination" and rule on whether a group of people could decide their own destiny, or have the course of their lives determined by others.

Madame Elysé was a witness for Mauritius, the African country for which I acted in the case. She would speak on behalf of Chagossians, in the language of Creole, delivered with clarity, force and passion. She could not read or write, so the judges agreed she would address them in a pre-recorded statement. She would watch them as they watched her, a woman in a black suit and a white shirt edged with lace, wearing a small blue and red badge that proclaimed: "Let Us Return!"

The President opened the proceedings with a short summary of the case, then invited the first speaker to address the Court. Slowly, Sir Anerood Jugnauth—eighty-eight years old, former Prime Minister of Mauritius, member of the Bar of England and Wales, Queen's Counsel—made his way to the podium. He spoke for exactly fifteen minutes, followed by two advocates, a short *pause café* and then a third advocate. He and the lawyers spoke from prepared scripts, which offered an air of theatre, the judges as audience. They did not interrupt, they did not ask questions.

I made my way to the podium. I had addressed the Court many times before, yet on this occasion was somehow more anxious. Madame Elysé, now in the front row, stood briefly as I introduced her. "The Court should hear the voice of the Chagossians directly," I explained, to obtain a sense of the realities of colonial rule.

Madame Elysé's statement was projected on two large screens that hung above the judges, words and images broadcast around the world. In faraway Port Louis, the capital of Mauritius, the proceedings were shown live on national television, as her friends gathered in a community centre to watch. They would weep as she spoke.

. . .

"Mappel Liseby Elysé."

"My name is Liseby Elysé." The translation appeared in English and French, neat captions in white at the bottom of the screen.

"I was born on 24 July 1953 in Peros Banhos. My father was born in Six Iles. My mother was born in Peros Banhos. My grandparents were also born there. I form part of the Mauritius delega-

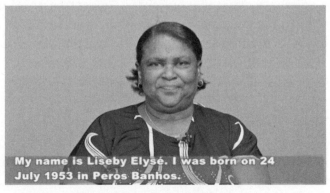

Liseby Elysé addresses the ICJ, 3 September 2018.

tion. I am telling how I have suffered since I have been uprooted from my paradise island. I am happy that the International Court is listening to us today. And I am confident that I will return to the island where I was born."

With these opening words, the mood in the Great Hall changed, as a heavy silence was felt, one that accompanies a significant moment in a public space, of the kind encountered in a theatre or a concert hall when a performer connects with an audience whose attention is fixed and keen. As Madame Elysé spoke, without a script, the President looked towards her, seated a few feet away, as memories tumbled out, words rough and powerful that cut through the pomp of the Great Hall:

"Everyone had a job, his family and his culture. But all that we ate was fresh food. Ships which came from Mauritius brought all our goods. We received our groceries. We received all that we needed. We did not lack anything. In Chagos everyone lived a happy life."

The tone changed, becoming less soft:

"One day the administrator told us that we had to leave our island, leave our houses and go away. All persons were unhappy. They were angry that we were told to go away. But we had no choice. They did not give us any reason. Up to now we have not been told why we had to leave. But afterwards ships which used to bring food stopped coming. We had nothing to eat. No medicine. Nothing at all. We suffered a lot. But then one day, a ship called *Nordvaer* came."

Madame Elysé paused:

"The administrator told us we had to board the ship, leaving everything, leaving all our personal belongings behind except a few clothes and go. People were very angry about that and when this was done, it was done in the dark."

She paused again as a frown passed across her brow. She did not name the administrator—Monsieur Willis-Pierre Prosper—or the date, which was 27 April 1973, in the evening, at dusk:

"We boarded the ship in the dark so that we could not see our island. And when we boarded the ship, conditions in the hull of the ship were bad. We were like animals and slaves in that ship. People were dying of sadness in that ship."

"Animals." "Slaves." Madame Elysé spat the words out:

"And as for me I was four months pregnant at that time. The ship took four days to reach Mauritius. After our arrival, my child was born and died. Why did my child die? For me, it was because I was traumatised on that ship, I was very worried, I was upset. This is why when my child was born, he died."

She drew her lips together:

"I maintain we must not lose hope. We must think one day will come when we will return on the land where we were born. My heart is suffering, and my heart still belongs to the island where I was born."

Imperceptibly, the camera closed in, emphasising the determination and rising anger:

"Nobody would like to be uprooted from the island where he was born, to be uprooted like animals. And it is heartbreaking. And I maintain justice must be done."

She seemed to struggle, to rein in the emotions, to keep a deep well of anger at bay, yet she was not able to stop herself. It was as if decades of emotion, anger and hope were unleashed:

"I must return to the island where I was born. Don't you feel that it is heartbreaking when someone is uprooted from his island like an animal and he does not know where he is being brought?"

Madame Elysé's voice broke, a tremolo across the silence:

"And I am very sad. I still don't know how I left my Chagos. They expelled us by force. And I am very sad."

She stopped and closed her eyes:

"My tears keep rolling every day. I keep thinking I must return to my island."

Then, at last, she let herself go:

"I maintain I must return to the island where I was born and I must die there and where my grandparents have been buried. In the place where I took birth, and in my native island."

She took a long breath, exhaled, swept her hand across her face, as if a great cleansing motion, looked into the camera, turned, allowed her head to drop. She wept. How might the judges react to so open and unusual an expression of emotion in so venerable a place of justice?

. . .

Madame Elysé spoke for three minutes and forty-seven seconds.
The silence that followed seemed interminable. As I stood at the

podium, a gentle sound filled the Great Hall of Justice, the sound of tears.

I waited to address the Court.

Later, after the morning session was over, as Madame Elysé and I stood outside the Great Hall, she turned to me with a sense of relief, a warm smile etched across her face.

"Did it go well?"

"Yes."

"May I ask a question?"

"Yes."

"Why did it take so long for us to come to The Hague?"

PART ONE

———•◆•———

1945

"The individual human being . . . is the ultimate unit of all law."

—HERSCH LAUTERPACHT, 1943

To answer the question posed by Madame Elysé, it is necessary to go back to February 1945 and a winter's day in Cleveland, Ohio. Standing at another podium, Ralph Bunche delivered a passionate lecture to the city's Council on World Affairs, on colonialism and its future. Bunche, a US State Department official, was a Black American and a distinguished scholar of British and French administration in Africa. His lecture offered a robust response to an argument recently put to him by Arthur Creech Jones, the British Labour Party's expert on colonialism. Given a choice between slow progress under British domination, or freedom under new international rules, Creech Jones explained, the colonised would opt for the former. And, he added, Bunche should apply his dangerous ideas on decolonisation to himself and to the fifteen million Black people of the United States.

"The modern world has come to the realisation that there is a great moral issue involved in the perpetuation of the colonial system," Dr. Bunche declared in response. Is one people entitled to rule permanently over another? No. In the coming weeks he would have a chance to turn this idea into action, in negotiating a new international agreement, the Charter that would create the United Nations organisation and begin the

Ralph Bunche, 1951.

formal process of ending colonialism. Bunche spoke with authority, as the member of the US delegation negotiating the Charter,
charged with reaching agreement on decolonisation. A few weeks
later, in April 1945, as work on the international agreement began
in earnest at the San Francisco Opera House, he wrote to his wife.
"I did feel a bit proud this afternoon, at being the only Negro who
sat on the first floor."

The drafting process lasted eight weeks, the result reflected in
Chapter XI of the UN Charter, a "Declaration Regarding Non-
Self-Governing Territories." Possibly the "most far-reaching declaration on colonial history ever written," one delegate called it.
Bunche recognised the limits of his efforts, expressing the hope
that the new rules would be taken forward and implemented in
good faith. He could not know that his work would unlock a door
through which Madame Elysé would pass, many decades later, on
a journey from Chagos to The Hague.

NEWFOUNDLAND

The origins of Chapter XI of the UN Charter and its commitment to decolonisation may be traced back to earlier revolutionary
moments, in America and France and other places, to philosophical
and political writings on the relationship between a person and the
larger community of which they form a part. Such ideas prompted
Vladimir Ilyich Lenin to publish three articles on "The Right of
Nations to Self-Determination," a call to end external domination.
Four years later, American President Woodrow Wilson addressed
the US Congress with similar ideas, touching on the interests of
colonised populations. One of his Fourteen Points invoked the
principle of "autonomous development" for different peoples of
the Austro-Hungarian and Ottoman empires, the idea that each
national group might have rights of its own. Such ideas influenced
other thinkers, like W.E.B. Du Bois and Eliézer Cadet, and the

Universal Negro Improvement Association founded by Marcus Garvey. In the post-war years, they pushed for the "right of self-determination" to be "applied to Africans and to every European colony where the African race predominates," and for Germany's African colonies to be returned to "the natives."

Two decades later, in 1941, as war raged once more, German forces headed into Soviet territory and the lands of north Africa. They threatened British control of Egypt and the Suez Canal, the route to Mauritius, India and other colonial domains. In the east, Japan posed its own threat to British, Dutch and French colonies. Not yet engaged in the war, President Franklin Delano Roosevelt used this moment to propose a meeting with British Prime Minister Winston Churchill. "Somewhere in the Atlantic," Churchill whispered, a secret location.

The two met on Saturday, 9 August 1941, on board the USS *Augusta*, moored in Little Placentia Sound, off the coast of New-foundland, a British colony. The following day, they discussed the draft of a joint statement they might issue. Over dinner, Roosevelt's son, Captain Elliot Roosevelt of the US Army Air Force, observed a "highly charged" quarrel between FDR and Churchill, on colonialism and the British Empire. Roosevelt provoked Churchill, telling him he wanted to end preferential trade and other economic arrangements for Britain's colonies.

"England does not propose for a moment to lose its favoured position among the British Dominions," Churchill responded, irritated. Roosevelt countered: real peace required the "development of backward countries," and, to confront fascism, the two countries must work together to free people from "a backward colonial policy."

Churchill's effort to change the subject was unsuccessful. The United States would not underwrite colonialism, Roosevelt continued, and would support "popular movements" for independence and self-government. As we look back to the Cold War years that followed, to developments in Chile, Nicaragua, Iraq and Afghanistan, among others, the charge of hypocrisy can easily be levelled against the US. Nevertheless, Roosevelt hoped to replace British colonialism with a New American Century, and one of his ideas would be taken forward as the "principle of self-determination."

Robust views were exchanged over several days. The Americans arrived with a draft text, but Roosevelt did not share it with Churchill, fearing it would be rejected outright. Better to allow the British to prepare a draft of their own, to which the Americans could respond. The ploy worked. The first draft of the "Atlantic Charter," Churchill would say, was "a British production cast in my own words."

He walked straight into the trap laid by Roosevelt.

The draft was reworked, words added or changed, or removed. Sentences were inserted, new points raised. After three days, the two agreed on a short text that set out their hopes for a "better future for the world." The ideas included respect for territory; more economic cooperation; an end to trade preferences for the colonies; individual freedoms; and limits on the use of military force.

The Atlantic Charter was a single typewritten page consisting of eight brief paragraphs. In due course, paragraph three would become crucial for Mauritius and Madame Elysé, the words that committed Britain and America to "respect the right of all peoples to choose the form of government under which they will live." The idea was revolutionary, invoking the notion that sovereign rights and self-government would be "restored to those who have been forcibly deprived of them." Churchill wrote the words without thinking through how they might be interpreted and applied.

The Atlantic Charter was widely reported in the press. A statement of intentions, *The New Yorker* magazine noted, and a pretty good one, even if open to interpretation. Roosevelt saw the Charter as announcing an end to empire, taking forward Wilson's Fourteen Points, a tool that promised people in the east of Europe "their own nation-state."

Churchill read the text differently. No, he assured the House of Commons, the Atlantic Charter did not imply an end to Britain's colonies—its vital third paragraph was only for those who lived "under the Nazi yoke." Those who owed allegiance to the Crown, in India, Burma, Mauritius and other parts of the British Empire, would not be subject to the commitment expressed in the third paragraph.

Churchill's reading was not so widely shared. Across Africa, many read the words of the third paragraph as applying to them and the colonies of their continent, a commitment for the "Africanization" of governments. In South Africa, a young Nelson Mandela saw the words of the Atlantic Charter not as empty promises, but as offering "full citizenship," the right to land and an end to "all discriminating legislation."

The world of international law was—and still is—conservative and cautious, but once words are agreed upon they often take on a life of their own. A few months after the Atlantic Charter was adopted, the third paragraph was picked up and its sentiment inserted into the "Declaration by the United Nations," adopted in Washington, DC, in January 1942. Twenty-six countries agreed to join forces against Germany and Japan, whose attack on Pearl Harbor, a month earlier, had prompted the Americans to enter the war. The Soviet Union and China were among the countries that embraced the Atlantic Charter's commitment to self-government, and called for the preservation of "human rights and justice in their own lands as well as in other lands."

Within a few years, some fifty countries were supporting the 1942 Declaration, with four from Africa: Egypt, Ethiopia, Liberia and South Africa. The commitment to decolonisation had taken off, even if the modalities were uncertain.

In February 1945 at the Yalta Conference, where Churchill, Roosevelt and Stalin met to discuss the defeat of Germany and arrangements for the post-war world, Churchill again objected to Roosevelt's efforts to subject British colonies to international rules and scrutiny. "I will have no suggestion that the British Empire is to be put into the dock and examined by everybody to see that it is up to their standard," the Prime Minister told Stalin. "Never, Never, Never . . . every scrap of territory over which the British flag flies is immune."

The US led the effort to create a new organisation, the United Nations. The Secretary of State wanted someone with commitment, and a knowledge of Africa, to lead on decolonisation. "We want to employ for the future colonial problems of this international organization the best qualified man, who happens to be a Negro," explained the secretary general of the conference on the United Nations. That man was Ralph Bunche, a political scientist who worked on colonialism at the State Department, a staunch supporter of decolonisation and self-determination, drawing from his own experiences of racial prejudice in the United States.

In June 1945, a month after the war's end in Europe, fifty countries signed the Charter of the United Nations, filling the gap left by the demise of the League of Nations. This Charter established a Security Council, a powerful organ of fifteen members—five would be permanent (the United States, Britain, France, China and the Soviet Union), the other ten elected for two years—to maintain international peace and security. Other UN organs included a General Assembly of the entire membership, as the "main deliberative and policy-making organ," and a new International Court of Justice, as the principal judicial organ of the UN. Fifteen judges at the Peace Palace in The Hague would resolve contentious disputes between states. (In May 1947, Britain filed the first case, alleging that Albania had laid mines in the Corfu Channel in violation of international law and the "dictates of humanity.") The judges were also empowered to give advisory opinions "on any legal question," if requested by the Security Council or General Assembly.

The Americans pushed for decolonisation in the UN Charter, albeit with another name. The "hardest working conference I ever

attended," Ralph Bunche would call it, with trusteeship and decolonisation the "hottest" subject of all, a "tough fight at every step."
He largely succeeded: decolonisation became a fundamental aim of
the United Nations, as Article 1 of the Charter committed members
to respect "the principle of . . . self-determination of peoples." The
words were bold and significant, the language a compromise, a nod
to the British and French, fearful about the loss of colonies. "Not
as good as I would like it to be," Bunche reported, "but better than
any of us expected it could get."

The Charter made no mention of colonies. Instead, Chapter
XI referred to "Non-Self-Governing Territories," a less inflam-
matory and more acceptable formulation for anxious Europeans.
Article 73 imposed responsibilities on those who administered territories "whose peoples have not yet attained full self-government":
the colonisers must recognise the interests and well-being of the
colonised as "paramount," and promote self-government by the
local inhabitants. How this would occur depended on the particular state of "advancement" of each colony. The Charter created a
new international Trusteeship System, to administer other areas,
known as "trust territories," under the responsibility of a Trusteeship Council.

In this way, the UN Charter created a framework for change,
an embryonic commitment to decolonisation. The text reflected a
deal, an agreement to disagree, the United States on one side, Britain on the other. Yet it was a start and, as with so much in life, once
an idea is off the ground, there may be no stopping it.

DEPORTATION

As the paramount interests of the colonised came to the fore, other
developments in international law sought to promote the rights of
individuals and groups. A new human rights system emerged, as
governments committed themselves to a range of ideas, including

the right of people not to be forcibly removed from their homes and transferred to other places.

A catalyst for change was National Socialism and its idea of *Lebensraum*, the creation of more "living spaces" for Germans of Aryan descent across occupied Europe. *Lebensraum* was brutal, with local inhabitants rounded up, deported and replaced by German colonists. The terrible human consequences informed the drafters of the Nuremberg Statute, gathered in London in the summer of 1945 to create the world's first international criminal tribunal, with the power to prosecute senior Nazi leaders for "crimes against humanity." The legal concept was promoted by Hersch Lauterpacht, a Cambridge academic, whose new book on an international bill of rights of man offered a blueprint for the Universal Declaration on Human Rights.

"Crimes against humanity" at Nuremberg included "deportation," the forcible transfer of a group from one territory to another. This was a subject of personal interest, as I wrote in *East West Street*: two of my great-grandmothers, elderly widows, were deported from Vienna to Theresienstadt and Treblinka, respectively, where they perished. Each was allowed a single suitcase. The charges against many of the Nazi defendants at Nuremberg included their role in supporting *Lebensraum* as part of Germany's "new order," one intended to dismantle British colonies in Africa and elsewhere, while colonising Poland and other European territories.

In his opening arguments to the Nuremberg Tribunal, in November 1945, US prosecutor Robert Jackson addressed the subject of deportations and Nazi colonies, and the idea of "a right of self-determination" for Germans. Jackson contrasted Germany's behaviour with "legitimate" British and French approaches to colonialism; the latter was obtained, he asserted, without recourse to "aggressive warfare." Sir Hartley Shawcross, the British prosecutor, emphasised the legitimacy of the British Empire, and Germany's war against it. In October 1946, nine of the twenty-four defendants were convicted of crimes against humanity, including for their roles in deportations. Seven were hanged.

In this way, the Nuremberg trial catalysed new principles which would take root across time and place, as deportation became recognised as a "crime against humanity." Broadly, this is how international law works: someone develops an idea, puts it into writing (in an article or a book, perhaps); it germinates into an agreed legal text, migrates into another legal text, and then develops a life of its own as judges interpret and apply the words. The ideas of the three Charters—Atlantic, UN, Nuremberg—cross-fertilised, percolated elsewhere and, eventually, would reach the judges.

In December 1946, the UN General Assembly, at its first ever meeting, resolved that deportation was a "crime against humanity." Two years later, in December 1948, in Paris, the Assembly adopted the Universal Declaration of Human Rights. Silent on self-determination and colonialism, the Declaration nevertheless recognised that each of us, as individual human beings, has the right "to return to his country."

The following summer, governments met in Geneva to sign a new international agreement on war crimes, to offer greater protections to civilians in times of war. The 1949 Geneva Convention explicitly prohibited the "forcible transfer" of individuals or groups, or their deportation from one territory to another. The Red Cross hoped the new rules would end for all time the "hateful" act of deportation. Britain actively supported the development and was one of the first countries to sign the treaty.

The post-war years were momentous, as foundations were laid for a new legal order. In 1950, Ralph Bunche became the first Black person to be awarded the Nobel Peace Prize; in colonised Mauritius he was a figure of inspiration for university students. That year too, European countries signed the European Convention on Human Rights, the first treaty allowing individuals to enforce rights against their own states before an international court.

Britain supported the Convention, which entered into force in 1953. However, London was careful to exclude Mauritius from the colonies to which the Convention applied, so that those who lived there, including on Peros Banhos and other islands of Chagos, had no rights under it or its later protocols. One of these protocols would, in due course, explicitly prohibit any person from being expelled from the territory of the state of which they were a national. Britain never signed it.

Around the time the European Convention became binding on Britain, a child was born to Marcelle and Charles Bertrand, who lived on Île du Coin, one of the many islands of Peros Banhos and Chagos. She was baptised in the island's only church, with its white brick walls and bright red roof. Liseby, as she was named, was a child of colonialism, a subject of British rule but with far fewer rights than those who administered her place of birth.

PEROS BANHOS

Peros Banhos comprises three dozen islands and islets, seven of which were inhabited when Liseby Bertrand was born in the summer of 1953. Île du Coin was the most populous, a speck of sand and coconut trees, home to some 400 souls.

By the time of Liseby's birth, Peros Banhos had been a British colony for a century and a half, administered as a dependency of Mauritius. It was ruled from London, a consequence of the Treaty of Paris, signed in May 1814, which ended the Napoleonic Wars, prohibited international trade in slaves, and ceded various French colonies to Britain. One was Île de France, known by the British as Mauritius, a larger island created by volcanic activity that became a British colony along with numerous of its dependencies, including the Chagos Archipelago. Peros Banhos was 2,000 kilometres from Île de France, and five times that distance from London and Paris. The nearest place was the Maldives, some 500 kilometres away, a British protectorate.

Liseby was born a British colonial subject as an accident of history. She could have been Portuguese, as her island was reputedly claimed in 1513 by Afonso de Albuquerque, a navigator and governor of Portuguese India. It was said by some to have been named in honour of Pêro dos Banhos, a Portuguese explorer who perished there in 1555 when his ship, the *Conceição*, ran aground, although doubts have been expressed as to the true location of the atoll in the account of the tragedy recorded by Manuel Rangel, a mariner, in his *A tragedia dos Baixos de Pêro dos Banhos*. Rangel recorded the travails of the 165 voyagers who survived the wreck, including two women and five Catholic priests, stranded on a small, flat island, populated by coconut trees and grasses, with drinking water nestled in shallow wells carved into the sand, a home for turtles and thousands of birds. To their surprise, they were later and elsewhere greeted by a "group of black people" with boats.

In due course the Dutch took possession of Chagos, including the island known as Peros Banhos, holding on until 1769, when France claimed Diego Garcia, the largest of the islands. Monsieur Pierre Marie Normande, a Frenchman, was granted a concession to run a coconut plantation, producing generous quantities of copra, the succulent flesh of dried coconuts, with the assistance of enslaved people introduced from the places today called Mozambique and Madagascar, on the east coast of southern Africa. The enslaved, who included Madame Elysé's ancestors, worked the copra to produce a valuable oil.

In 1810 the British evicted the French from Île de France. Four years later, the territory was formally ceded to Britain, along with Chagos. Within a year, trade in enslaved people was formally prohibited on every possession, dominion and dependency of Her Majesty's Government, even the most "remote and minute." The enslaved of Peros Banhos obtained a degree of formal freedom, although whether they noticed a change in their actual conditions is not recorded.

The British remained, and during the Second World War the

islands of Chagos offered fuelling stations for warships. By 1945, when "self-determination" was written into the UN Charter, Chagos's inhabitants—comprising the *ilois*, born on the islands, and contract workers—mostly worked for the *Société Huilière de Diego et Peros*, which offered employment and shelter to the oil workers, and education for their children.

It is not easy to glean much information about Peros Banhos from that time, and few photographs remain. One shows the waterfront of Île du Coin, around the time Madame Elysé was born, offering clues about life on the island. Two white men amble along the concrete jetty; one has a hat and holds a camera. Iron rails run along the jetty, on which a fishing net is laid out. A wooden boat approaches, carrying four bare-chested Black men. An electricity cable hangs from wooden poles. A policeman walks away from the photographer, in a pale-coloured uniform. His belt, peak cap and truncheon offer signs of colonial authority.

Another photograph shows the island manager's house, three storeys painted white. It has a veranda, and two large stone pillars

Peros Banhos, 1960s.

announce the entrance, with a staircase to the upper floor. Four visitors stand near the building, white people, close to an enclosed area of grass, with two wooden benches. Coconut trees bend in the wind, a flower bed is neatly manicured. The impression is of order and tranquillity, the serenity of colonial authority.

A third photograph depicts the interior of the small church where Madame Elysé was baptised, rows of wooden benches under a beamed roof. A statue of Jesus stands with arms outstretched, along with two other statues, of garlanded ladies with hands clasped and beatific faces. The walls are painted and cracked, lined with shadows and mildew. On the altar stand two vases, holding simple floral arrangements.

These are portraits of colonial power and religious devotion, with modern conveniences, like electricity and transport, a sense of habitability as Britain's empire unravelled. Transjordan was the first of Britain's colonies to go, soon after the Second World War, then India, with much bloodshed, splintered initially into two countries, and later a third. Momentum gathered: the British mandate in Palestine was terminated; Burma and Ceylon gained independence; Newfoundland entered a union with Canada; Libya, after Italian colonial rule, passed from British and French control to independence; Eritrea merged with Ethiopia.

Large parts of Africa remained under colonial rule. France, Spain, Portugal and Belgium, and Britain too, held on to their distant possessions and subjects. In Mauritius, the British governor, Sir Hilary Rudolph Robert Blood, was comfortably ensconced in his "pocket handkerchief paradise," as he called it.

This was the world on 24 July 1953, the day that Liseby Bertrand was born, about seven weeks after the coronation of Elizabeth II, her Queen. In London, the American singer Frankie Laine's "I Believe" had just been knocked off the top of the charts.

LISEBY, 1953

Liseby is a fine recounter of stories, and I enjoyed her tales, with their clear, rich narrative structures, offering a collective memory of people and place:

"I was born in 1953, on the Île du Coin, a part of Peros Banhos. My father was Charles Bertrand. He was thirty-five years old, born in 1917, on 26 April. He was born on Six Iles, which the English called Egmont Islands. He was a baker, he made bread for the workers of the Société Huilière de Diego et Peros, the company that ran the coconut plantations which made copra, which produced oil.

In the 1960s, when I was a child, the company was bought by the Chagos Agalega Company, based in the Seychelles. I think it was run by Monsieur Moulinié. On the side, my father also worked as a gardener, he produced vegetables.

My mother was Marcelle, from the family Antalika. She was younger than my father, she was born in the 1930s, I don't know which year. Like me, she was born on Peros Banhos, on the Île du Coin. She looked after the children. There were seven of us: me, my five brothers—Alexis, France, Hervé, Cyril and Sylvie, who we call Toto—and my sister Ailine. Like all Chagossian women, my mother also worked in copra, for the plantation.

Where did we live? Like everyone, in a hut, with walls made of wood and straw. The roof was also straw, laid with leaves of coconut plants. We had no electricity and no running water. We would get all the water we needed from a well, to cook and to clean. It was fine. We had everything we needed.

I do not know so much about my family background. My father often liked to tell us stories about the family. He spoke in Creole, that was the language we spoke, and which I still speak. He talked often of his parents, and although I don't remember my grandmother, I heard a lot about her from his stories.

My father would tell us how white people had come to the islands, bringing with them Black people. He said our ancestors came from Mozambique, that they were slaves, but I have no proof of that, no details. In fact, I have no idea when my ancestors first arrived. I do not have a date, and no year was ever mentioned to me. My father just told us many stories, how he said we arrived on the island.

We were Catholic, and religious. Every Sunday we went to mass, in the church on Île du Coin. It was a small white church, a lovely place. Sometimes a priest would come from Mauritius, maybe every three months, or perhaps less often, every six months. Mostly, if there was no priest, the island administrator would celebrate the mass. His name was Monsieur Robert Talbot. He was a Mauritian, and I think his brother was born on Peros Banhos.

Monsieur Talbot lived in the big house, more than one floor, the one in the photograph. There was a long staircase that led to the entrance. It was near the church. He lived there until the islands were taken over by the English company. That was later in the 1960s, I think."

The village was well served. There was a shop, hangars for boats and the wood joinery, a stable, a blacksmith, a prison, a chapel and a mission, and a mill. There were small factories, a station to generate electricity, cow and sea-turtle pens, a slaughterhouse and a pier, with a flagpole for the Union Jack. There was a hospital and a football pitch, and a school had opened in 1956.

"When I was seven years old my mother fell ill. Our family travelled together to Mauritius, by boat, to Port Louis. We stayed there for some time, but my mother did not get better. She died. I returned with my father to Peros Banhos. I stayed at the school, which had opened a few years earlier, for another two years, but that stopped when I was nine years old. I had not learned to read

or write. That was when I started to work, helping my father in
the garden, with his vegetables.

I was very happy as a child. I remember Peros Banhos as a
paradise. We had everything we needed. We had shelter and water.
We had friends and family. We had food. There was fish, and the
vegetables that my father grew, and we had chickens."

Liseby has no photographs of herself in Peros Banhos, but her
nephew Olivier Bancoult showed me others that offered a sense of
the period. She was too young to recall the visit to Peros Banhos in
1955 by the British Governor, Sir Robert Scott. Arriving in a feath-
ered hat, he was greeted on the quay by children who sang "God
Save the Queen" and waved little Union Jacks. In the "go-down,"
where food products were stored, his team projected a Charlie
Chaplin film, and another with Johnny Weissmuller in the role of
Tarzan.

"What else do I remember best from my childhood? I loved climb-
ing the trees, the moringa trees. I think you call them drumstick

Peros Banhos, 1960s.

tree, because of the seedpods, which hang from the branches. We cooked the leaves of the moringa in coconut milk, or we made a soup with them, with oil and onion and garlic. We liked to play with the seedpods, *les batons mouroum* we called them, the drumsticks. We made music with the drumsticks. I remember the music. Every Saturday night there was a dance, for the whole of the community, all of us together. We called it *la soirée*. We had our own music and songs, we loved to sing. We danced. We loved to dance, late into the night.

Then one day everything changed."

PART TWO

1966

"The object is to frighten him with hope."

—NOTE TO HAROLD WILSON, September 1965

Monday, 18 July 1966, three o'clock. Fourteen judges of the International Court of Justice entered the Great Hall of Justice to deliver judgements in two important cases, brought by Liberia and Ethiopia against South Africa. Thousands of miles away, on Peros Banhos, Liseby Bertrand prepared to celebrate her thirteenth birthday, blissfully unaware of the colonial battle being fought in The Hague.

The cases were brought to hold South Africa to account for its racial mistreatment of the inhabitants of South West Africa—today Namibia—and its refusal to allow the former colony to become an independent country. Six years earlier, the UN General Assembly had passed resolution 1514, the "Declaration on the Granting of Independence to Colonial Countries and Peoples."

The Court's President back then was Sir Percy Spender, a former Australian Foreign Minister and ambassador to the United States. Spender was seen as self-made, able, energetic, elegantly abrasive, with a white handkerchief permanently in the breast pocket of his jacket, and a neatly trimmed moustache. Elected as a judge at the Court in the late 1950s, he was a man of his times on matters of colonialism and race, a "classic homo americanus," open to the spirit of the Atlantic Charter but resistant to any real change on colonial matters. He vigorously defended Australia's administration of Papua and New Guinea, and opposed the decolonisation of Western New Guinea by the Dutch, believing the colonisers would better serve the interests of the Indigenous people than Indonesia.

He enjoyed life and travels, the annual trip home from The

Sir Percy Spender, President, ICJ, 1966.

Hague, with convenient breaks, sometimes in the British colony of Mauritius, a place he liked. One vacation was spent on a former plantation in South Carolina: the guests were assisted by horses, dogs and "Negro grooms," his wife recorded in a memoir, and by "other Negroes whose duties I never succeeded in working out."

On this day of judgement, in the summer of 1966, in the Palace of Peace, Sir Percy read out the two rulings that would spark outrage across the globe. The words he spoke would damage his—and the Court's—reputation forever. To understand the gulf between Sir Percy's view of the world, and the world's view of the words he would read out, it is necessary to go back to a moment in New York, six years earlier.

RESOLUTION 1514

Liseby Bertrand was seven years old in the autumn of 1960, a young child in an evolving world. "The wind of change is blowing through this continent," declared British Prime Minister Harold Macmillan in Cape Town, South Africa, as ever more countries obtained independence. "We must all accept it as a fact, and our national policies must take account of it."

Sixteen African countries joined the UN that year, although Mauritius was not one of them. At the General Assembly, committees on decolonisation reviewed lengthy reports from the colonial powers on the steps they claimed to be taking for the people of non-self-governing territories, as the colonies were called. Britain's report on Mauritius included information on Chagos and its "Oil Islands," as they were known, including Peros Banhos—Britain was not planning to leave Mauritius anytime soon.

Decolonisation was not to everyone's liking as colonial matters rose up the agenda of international affairs. A British delegate to the UN complained that much debate was based on emotion rather than reason. This reflected, he noted in a communication to London, a form of "colour prejudice in reverse," an unjustified "resentment of the darker peoples against the past domination of the world by European nations."

Publicly, the United States claimed to be supportive of the winding down of the old colonial powers, yet behind the scenes the position was different. As the Cold War raged, the Soviets were seen to pose an increasing threat, which gave rise to a connection being drawn in Washington between "colonial questions" at the UN and matters of national security. In the late 1950s, the US started to plan for new military bases around the world, some of which could be located on obscure atolls, as part of a "worldwide contest between the free and the Communist worlds." Such bases had to remain in the hands of friends, which meant the colonial powers in Africa.

In the autumn of 1960, "self-determination" reached the floor of the General Assembly. Inspired by the words of the UN Charter prepared by Ralph Bunche, the moment was catalysed by the Afro-Asian Conference held in Bandung, Indonesia, five years earlier: twenty-nine countries, meeting as the newly created Non-Aligned Movement, declared colonialism to be "an evil," one to be ended "speedily." They called for the principle of self-determination to be applied to all peoples and nations.

The Bandung declaration led directly to the General Assembly in New York. In the summer of 1960, various drafts of a resolution circulated under the wing of Frederick Boland, an Irish diplomat who served as President of the Assembly that year. Born into a British colony—Ireland obtained independence in May 1921, when the island was divided, with Northern Ireland retained by Britain—Boland was a fearless supporter of decolonisation. Living with him was his daughter Eavan, later a writer of renown. "What is a colony?" one of her poems would inquire.

World leaders travelled to New York to discuss decolonisation. Nikita Khrushchev, the Soviet leader, offered a far-reaching draft. President Dwight D. Eisenhower recognised the drive for self-determination, but did not offer clear support for the idea. British Prime Minister Harold Macmillan was cautious, able to recognise a goal of "political independence" for Africa without offering any specific details or commitments. This was an age of uprisings and national liberation movements, in Asia and Africa, but also in Europe. Iran, Cyprus, Algeria and Kenya were among the many places where civil unrest was being fomented.

Delegates from Africa and Asia spoke strongly for decolonisation, supported by a handful of Europeans, led by delegates from Cyprus and Ireland. "My country has not yet recovered its 'historic unity,'" the Irish delegate stated, expressing support for the integrity of colonial territories, the idea that no colony could be dismembered in the period before independence. He expressed the hope that Ireland would soon recover its unity (six decades later, the wish remains unfulfilled, although fulfilment may be on the horizon).

American, Honduran and Soviet draft resolutions fell by the wayside, leaving just a single text, one proposed by forty-three African and Asian countries for a "Declaration on the Granting of Independence to Colonial Countries and Peoples." The vote took place on the afternoon of 14 December 1960: eighty-nine countries voted in favour of resolution 1514, none voted against. Nine countries abstained (largely the colonisers, like Britain and France, but also a couple of former colonies—Australia and the Dominican Republic). The US State Department hoped to support the draft, but a last-minute intervention by President Eisenhower ordered an abstention, reportedly at the request of Harold Macmillan.

Resolution 1514 was short, just a few paragraphs. "All peoples have the right to self-determination," it declared, with domination and exploitation by one country of another to be regarded as a denial of fundamental human rights. The resolution proclaimed a principle of "territorial integrity," to prohibit "any attempt aimed at the partial or total disruption of the territorial integrity" of a colonised country.

A chastened delegate explained Britain's abstention: his country could accept self-determination as a principle but not as a legal "right." On "territorial integrity" the British said nothing. Mr. Boland of Ireland, however, was unable to stop himself from expressing satisfaction with resolution 1514 and closed the session on an upbeat note: "The Assembly may well congratulate itself on this accomplishment."

SOUTH WEST AFRICA

As resolution 1514 was in train, Liberia and Ethiopia started legal proceedings in The Hague to challenge South Africa's rule over South West Africa. South West Africa had been colonised in the nineteenth century by Germany, whose brutal rule included the mass murder of the Herero people, an act that Germany has recently recognised as a genocide. During the First World War the territory was occupied by South Africa, and the League of Nations then conferred on Britain a mandate over the territory, to be exercised by its colony, South Africa. South West Africa became a colony of a colony.

After South Africa obtained its independence in 1931, its occupation of the territory continued. With the establishment of the United Nations and new rules on trusteeship and decolonisation, South Africa's activities in South West Africa came under increased scrutiny. South Africa wanted to continue its administration under the old rules of the League of Nations mandate, a means to avoid the new UN rules on fundamental human rights and decolonisation. South Africa's embrace of apartheid and racial segregation prompted the General Assembly to act, requesting an advisory opinion from the judges in The Hague on South Africa's obligations in respect of South West Africa.

In 1950 the Court gave its opinion, concluding that although South Africa's original mandate had not lapsed, it was required to report to the United Nations on its supervision of the territory. In short, the Court ruled, although South Africa did not have to subject South West Africa to the new UN rules, or follow the path to inevitable independence, it could not alter the status of the territory.

Five years later, the Court gave a second advisory opinion to the General Assembly of the UN. This confirmed the lawfulness of various decisions taken by the Assembly on the governance of South West Africa. A year later, in 1956, a third advisory opinion determined that people living in South West Africa had the right to complain directly to the UN about their treatment under apartheid and other South African measures.

By subjecting South Africa's exercise of power to constraints, the three advisory opinions enhanced the Court's position in the eyes of many African countries. Some started to see the Palace of Peace as "a place of progressive potential." Diligent readers of the Court's third opinion would note a clear warning from Judge Lauterpacht that South Africa's persistent disregard of General Assembly decisions could be illegal under international law. The General Assembly picked up on Lauterpacht's signal, calling on countries to think about bringing a case against South Africa, for its mistreatment of the inhabitants of South West Africa. The moment was propitious: South Africa resisted the "winds of change," outlawed the African National Congress (founded in 1912 to defend the rights and freedoms of Africans), and prosecuted Nelson Mandela for treason. At Sharpeville, where South African police fired on peaceful protesters, sixty-nine individuals were killed.

Liberia decided to sue South Africa. It retained the services of Ernest Gross, a former US State Department lawyer who had worked closely with Ralph Bunche at the UN; Ethiopia promptly followed suit with a second case. In November 1960, shortly before resolution 1514 was adopted, Liberia and Ethiopia filed their cases against South Africa in The Hague. Both had been members of the League of Nations: they wanted to end apartheid and the mistreatment of South West Africa's inhabitants, and challenge South Africa's refusal to countenance independence.

The Court joined the two cases, which South Africa argued should be thrown out on the basis that neither country had any legal interest in the treatment of the colony's inhabitants. By a narrow majority, in its 1962 judgement the Court rejected South Africa's jurisdictional challenge: eight of the fifteen judges ruled that Ethiopia and Liberia had "a legal right or interest" to protect the rights of the inhabitants. Seven judges dissented, led by the Australian, Sir Percy Spender, and his British colleague Sir Gerald Fitzmaurice, a former legal adviser at the Foreign Office. The two jointly wrote a bitter dissent, notable for its length and formalism. They argued that the Court had acted politically, by taking account of the "well-being and the social progress" of the colony's inhabitants. Such humanitarian instincts were outside the law and should not be addressed by an international court.

By the time the case reached the merits, Sir Percy had been elected President of the Court, with the active assistance of Judge Fitzmaurice. Spender was in some respects a moderniser—he introduced simultaneous interpretation between English and French, the Court's two languages, and public access to hearings—but he also kept a firm grip on matters of law and procedure. As the cases went through two rounds of written pleadings, and oral hearings that ran for more than twenty weeks, an issue arose as to the composition of the bench. Seventeen judges should have sat on the cases, the fifteen permanent judges and two *ad hoc* judges, one appointed by South Africa, the other by Liberia and Ethiopia. In the end, three of the seventeen judges did not participate in the judgements on the merits—one died, another fell ill, and the third was prevented from participating in a move apparently coordinated by Spender and Fitzmaurice.

The removal of the third judge, Sir Muhammad Zafarullah Khan, would prove to have huge consequences. Khan, from Pakistan, had represented the Muslim League on the decolonisation and partition of India, later serving as his country's first Foreign Minister. His first attempt to be elected to the Court had been unsuccessful, despite British support ("Head and shoulders above any candidate," a British official recorded, especially those from the "Mohammedan and Middle Eastern bloc"). Khan succeeded on a second attempt, in 1954, although by then the British had turned sharply against him (worried by what they saw as a "fanatical anti-colonial" stance).

As a judge on the Court, Sir Zafarullah Khan contributed to the South West Africa advisory opinions of 1955 and 1956. After his term of office ended in 1961, he returned to the UN as Pakistan's ambassador, serving as President of the General Assembly. In 1960 he declined an invitation from Ethiopia and Liberia to be appointed as *ad hoc* judge in the two cases in South West Africa. Four years later he was elected to serve a second term as a judge at the Court.

Sir Zafarullah Khan's election was not entirely welcome to Spender, who made clear to the Pakistani that he considered him to be conflicted from sitting on the cases, merely because Ethiopia and Liberia had wanted to appoint him as their *ad hoc* judge. When Khan told the Australian he saw no conflict of interest, since he had declined the appointment, Spender suggested that a "substantial majority" of the judges thought otherwise. "We will be appreciative of your decision" not to sit on the cases, Spender wrote, in effect forcing Sir Zafarullah's withdrawal, supported by Sir Gerald Fitzmaurice, who was no fan of Khan's. (A decade earlier, as a lawyer at the Foreign Office in London, Fitzmaurice had opposed Khan's candidacy to be a judge, on the grounds he was too independent, "extremely difficult to influence," and prone to "adhere to his own view in all circumstances.") Lady Spender considered Khan to be eloquent and an "old friend," even if too fond of quoting the Koran.

Faced with such pressure, Khan recused himself. The fourteen judges who ruled on the merits divided equally: seven supported the cases brought by Liberia and Ethiopia, seven opposed. Under the Court's rules this gave the President the casting vote. As Spender delivered the judgement, one diplomat present in the Great Hall could hardly believe what was being said as, forty minutes into the reading, it dawned on him that South Africa would win the case. As Spender articulated the Court's conclusion—Ethiopia and Liberia had no right to come to the Court to hold South Africa to account—a gasp was heard across the courtroom. Spender's final words summarised the ruling: "The Court, by the President's casting vote—the votes being equally divided—decides to reject the claims of the Empire of Ethiopia and the Republic of Liberia."

Remarkably, over the four years the case ran, Spender and Fitzmaurice were able to revisit the earlier 1962 judgement—in which they had failed to persuade a majority to throw the case out—and procure a ruling that two African countries had no legal interest in challenging white South Africa's racist and discriminatory actions against the Black inhabitants of its colony. Their thinking—that humanitarian considerations should be excluded from judicial process—now prevailed. The function of the Court was to apply legal rules, not moral precepts, Spender's majority ruled, and those rules meant that one country could not bring a case to the Court to protect the rights of people in another country: the idea of an "actio popularis" did not exist in international law. (Three years later, in another case, the Court reversed that ruling, stating that international law did recognise such a right, a decision that would pave the way, five decades later, for The Gambia to bring a case against Myanmar for alleged genocidal acts against the Rohingya community.)

Several judges in the South West Africa case wrote strong dissenting opinions. I recall, years later, as a student, reading the one written by Philip Jessup, the US judge, the first and only dissent he ever wrote: the ruling was a gross error, he believed, one that was "completely unfounded" on the law and facts, as Ethiopia and Liberia obviously had a legal interest and their claim should have succeeded. Jessup expressed hope for "the intelligence of a future day"; his words irritated Spender, who reprimanded him for expressing views on the merits after the Court ruled it had no jurisdiction.

. . .

The South West Africa judgements plunged the Court into an abyss of disrepute, from which it would not emerge for two decades. In the era of decolonisation, the judges were seen to strike a blow for colonial rule, leaving apartheid and discrimination in place. The government of South Africa celebrated as others bemoaned the Court for dispensing justice "according to a 'white man's' law." Some saw the decision as the international law equivalent of *Dred Scott*, the notorious US Supreme Court judgement ruling, a century earlier, that the word "people" in the US Constitution did not include Africans or those who were enslaved.

Sir Zafarullah Khan took the highly unusual step—for a judge— of speaking on the record to a newspaper. "There were no grounds for disqualifying me," he told the *Observer* in London. His words added to the sense of outrage, confirming that if he had sat the decision would have gone the other way. Many—including some of Ethiopia and Liberia's lawyers—considered the Court had turned itself into an instrument of colonialism and, in so doing, an anachronistic irrelevance.

Members of the UN moved the General Assembly to affirm that resolution 1514 gave the people of South West Africa an "inalienable right to self-determination, freedom and independence." With immediate effect, the General Assembly terminated the mandate conferred on Britain and exercised by South Africa, resolving that South West Africa would be governed directly by the UN. One hundred and fourteen countries voted in favour of that resolution, two voted against, and three abstained, one of which was Britain. The Assembly changed the territory's name to Namibia, appointing a Commissioner and Council to administer it until independence. A few weeks after the judgement, the General Assembly adopted the International Covenant on Civil and Political Rights, a far-reaching and legally binding human rights instrument of potentially global application. Article 1 affirmed "All peoples have the right of self-determination," and obliged all parties to give effect to that right.

The displeasure of the General Assembly was reflected in the next elections to the Court. Spender retired, to be succeeded by a Nigerian judge, handing a traditionally white Commonwealth seat to Black Africa. In her memoir, Lady Spender passed in silence over the painful episode of South West Africa. She did, however, mention one person whose actions and notoriety would, in later years, unwittingly allow the Court to repair the damage it had done to itself: she recounted the Spenders' visit to Nicaragua, where they were warmly received by the country's despotic leader, President Anastasio Somoza. In due course, the end of Somoza's rule in 1979 would open the door to another case at the Court. But that was for later. It was now 1968, a significant year for Mauritius.

SEPARATION

On 12 March 1968 most of Mauritius ceased to be a colony of Britain and became independent. The Union Jack was lowered at a ceremony at the Camp de Mars racecourse in Port Louis and a new flag raised, one with four bright colours: red for freedom, blue for the Indian Ocean, yellow to mark the light of independence, and green to represent the country's verdant wonders. Under the new constitution, Elizabeth II would serve as Queen of Mauritius, and Sir Seewoosagur Ramgoolam became the country's first Prime Minister.

The country's road to independence from 1945 had been laboured, as Britain resisted the words of the Atlantic and UN Charters. The colony's constitution was modestly reformed, creating new legislative and executive bodies, elected by a popular vote of those who could read and write simple sentences in English, French or Creole, the country's three languages. There were conferences and constitutional revisions, as the locals were given a little more power, while real authority was vested in the Governor and in London. In 1959 the legislative council and Dr. Ramgoolam demanded autonomy followed by independence.

By 1964, Britain still refused to offer a date for independence. There was a reason for this—a secret reason. The Mauritian leaders did not know, as they engaged with Britain, that London was privately plotting with Washington, which had an eye on some of Mauritius's more distant islands. Secret talks began in the spring of 1963, on the use by the Americans of "certain small British-owned islands in the Indian Ocean" for a new military base. Drawing on a "Strategic Island Concept" conjured up by Stuart Barber, a naval planner at the US Department of Defense, and implemented by Paul Nitze, Diego Garcia was identified as a desirable spot. The British duly surveyed the island as a potential "military communications station." In 1964 the Americans asked the British to consider emptying the island of Diego Garcia, by removing the inhabitants. The talks, held in absolute secrecy, aimed at "security of tenure" and a long-term lease.

Aware of the legal and political risks, the British nevertheless offered to do the necessary, "at HMG's expense." "We have the power to do this," a secret memorandum concluded, "but must avoid the charge that we are 'trafficking in Colonial territory,' or failing to have regard to the interests of the inhabitants." Fear of an adverse reaction at the UN was palpable. There would "still be a local population, albeit very small in number," another memorandum noted, so Britain might be criticised for creating a new colony.

Ever inventive, the civil servants and lawyers in London came up with a solution to get around the UN rules and resolution 1514. Criticism of Britain would lose its force if—a big "if"—a means could be found to secure the consent of the Mauritian leadership or, failing that, "at least their acquiescence." Another possibility was to "confront the Mauritians with a *fait accompli*," or just "tell them at the last moment what we are doing." Legal minds in London were instructed to concoct arrangements to avoid a charge of lawlessness.

The British and American collaborators duly came up with a plan based on consent: they would develop a joint facility but not disclose the idea to the Mauritians, and the Governor, Sir John Rennie, would initiate consultations with Dr. Ramgoolam, the Mauritian premier, in the hope of obtaining his consent. But Dr. Ramgoolam resisted, uneasy about the "detachment" of Chagos, and insisted the colony's territory be kept intact, as resolution 1514's principles of self-determination and territorial integrity required. Instead, he offered a "long-term lease." Without mentioning the involvement of the United States, Governor Rennie merely informed the Mauritians that certain Chagos islands were being assessed. The survey was carried out under the direction of Mr. Robert Newton, the colonial secretary of Mauritius, a keen birdwatcher. I "took the line with island Managers that in a scientific age there was a growing need for accurate scientific surveys," Newton explained, and offered "vague allusions to the developments in radio communications." Of a future US base he said nothing.

Newton proposed the detachment of Chagos from Mauritius, the removal of all fifty-five or more islands from "the unpredictable course of politics that tends to follow independence." He recommended that the archipelago become "direct dependencies of the British Crown," a new colony. Blatantly ignoring resolution 1514, Newton nevertheless recognised that detachment "would give rise to considerable political difficulties." It "would scarcely be politic to deprive Mauritius of its dependencies," he recorded, "without some *quid pro quo*." The British recognised Chagos as part of the territory of Mauritius.

In January 1965, the Americans confirmed they wanted the entire archipelago to be detached from Mauritius, not just Diego Garcia. "[F]ull detachment now might more effectively assure that Mauritian political attention, including any recovery pressure, is diverted from Diego Garcia over the long run." Three months later, London gave in to the Americans: having declined to engage Britain in Lyndon Johnson's Vietnam war, Prime Minister Harold Wilson agreed to press ahead with the Chagos project, "as rapidly as possible." Another secret note confirmed that the islands of Chagos were "legally part of the territory of the colony," so that the consent of the Mauritian leaders was necessary for legality. "Generous compensation" was mentioned, the sum of £10 million mooted.

In May, the United States agreed to offer financial support, but under conditions of "great secrecy," as the US Congress would raise questions. Governor Rennie was instructed to communicate the idea of detachment to the Mauritian leaders, so that Chagos would be established as a new and distinct territory. This would be done by an Order in Council rather than an Act of Parliament, to maintain secrecy and avoid scrutiny. The US role would be hidden.

Premier Ramgoolam and his colleagues were not positive. They opposed detachment and asked for time to consider the proposals. In September, they were invited to London to discuss independence, which Britain was not yet willing to offer. At the Lancaster House conference, negotiating positions hardened: the British would detach without consent, the Mauritians would agree to a lease but not detachment. The Mauritius delegation included Anerood Jugnauth, a young lawyer.

On 23 September, Wilson met Ramgoolam at 10 Downing Street, armed with a briefing paper that spelled out the desired outcome, in stark terms: "The object is to frighten him with hope: hope that he might get independence; fright lest he might not unless he is sensible about the detachment of the Chagos Archipelago." The paper suggested: "The Prime Minister may therefore wish to make some oblique reference to the fact that H.M.G. have the legal right to detach Chagos by Order in Council, without Mauritius consent but this would be a grave step."

Wilson set out the options to his counterpart: "The Premier and his colleagues could return to Mauritius either with Independence or without it . . . Diego Garcia could either be detached by Order in Council or with the agreement of the Premier and his colleagues. The best solution of all might be Independence and detachment by agreement . . ." Again, Ramgoolam was not persuaded, and suggested a lease. "Not acceptable," the British responded.

This was the context in which an "understanding" was reached on "detachment": Mauritius would get independence, with £3 million in compensation, and more for landowners and Chagossians who would be resettled. The British offered trade concessions on sugar imports, fishing rights around Chagos—"as far as practicable"—and access to the benefits of minerals or oil discovered around Chagos. The British agreed that if the need for the facilities disappeared, the islands should be returned to Mauritius.

Reluctantly, and under intense pressure, Ramgoolam discussed the matter with his colleagues. The next day, the British and the Americans were informed that Ramgoolam and a majority of his ministers present in London had agreed to the detachment, under these conditions. The British set out the next steps, in three phases:

following detachment, normal life would continue on Peros Banhos and other islands not immediately needed for defence facilities; the population of islands needed for defence purposes would be "cleared off"; and Diego Garcia would be emptied of all local civilian inhabitants.

On 24 September 1965—two days after Wilson's meeting with Ramgoolam—Britain announced the decision to grant independence to Mauritius. In November, Governor Rennie informed London that a majority of the Mauritian Council of Ministers had agreed to the detachment. The matter was now urgent: to avoid difficulties at the UN, the detachment must be completed "as soon as possible," because Britain was being censured for holding on to Aden and Rhodesia.

It was likely, Colonial Secretary Anthony Greenwood warned, that Chagos would "be added to the list of 'imperialist' measures for which we are attacked," and that Britain would be accused of "creating a new colony in a period of decolonisation and of establishing new military bases when we should be getting out of the old ones." Speed and secrecy were vital, as delay would "jeopardise" the plan. The General Assembly was about to discuss Mauritius, and if the Mauritians learned of the deal with the United States, Britain would come under great pressure to withdraw the agreement. Moreover, Greenwood added, we would "lay ourselves open to an additional charge of dishonesty" if Britain evaded the issue in UN committees and then took its decision. His solution? "Present the UN with a *fait accompli*." Bypass Parliament, adopt the Order in Council, detach the islands, create "a separate colony," and do it now.

The Foreign Office concurred. The British mission in New York was instructed to "concert tactics" with the Americans and proceed on the basis of a big lie, telling the UN that the Chagos islands "have virtually no permanent Inhabitants." Lord Caradon, the British ambassador in New York, was uncomfortable with the use of the word "virtually." If the truth emerged that Chagos had any population, however small, there would be "charges of failure to carry out our Charter obligations to those who are permanent inhabitants." It would be preferable, Caradon advised, to proceed on the basis that there were "no permanent inhabitants." The word "virtually" was removed.

Some of the lawyers in London, the guardians of the rule of law, were less than comfortable. "This is really fairly unsatisfactory," warned one Foreign Office adviser. "We detach these islands—in itself a matter which is criticised"—then resettle the inhabitants or certify ("more or less fraudulently") that they belong somewhere else, an approach that could hardly be reconciled with the UN rules, Mr. Darwin wrote. Another lawyer, however, was entirely comfortable with a wholesale deportation, on the basis of a fiction that Chagos's inhabitants did not live there permanently. This was "the most desirable solution to the BIOT [British Indian Ocean Territory] problem," Mr. Aust advised, from the legal, financial and UN point of view. There was "nothing wrong in law or in principle" with total deportation, as Britain could "make up the rules as we go along" and treat the inhabitants as "not 'belonging'" to Chagos, in any sense.

On the morning of 8 November the Privy Council in London made an Order in Council to establish a new "British Indian Ocean Territory," encompassing all the islands of the Chagos Archipelago. A "BIOT" Commissioner was given far-reaching legal powers, including the forcible removal of the entire local population. The Order in Council changed the constitution of Mauritius, by removing Chagos from the definition of the colony's territory.

Despite the careful plans, news leaked out and reached New York, prompting an immediate, harsh reaction. The General Assembly quickly passed a resolution on Mauritius, expressing "deep concern" about the detachment of Chagos, instructing Britain not to "dismember" the territory and "violate its territorial integrity," and putting it on notice of future difficulties. Britain ignored it. A second resolution followed a year later, which was also ignored. Ten days later, Britain exchanged notes with the United States on an *Agreement Concerning the Availability for Defense Purposes of the British Indian Ocean Territory*. This declared "BIOT" to be British and available for the defence needs of both countries for fifty years, until 2016, to be extended for another twenty if necessary, until 2036. No user fee would be charged to the US. It was a very British gift.

In the summer of 1967, the UN's Committee of Twenty-Four deplored the "dismemberment of Mauritius," a clear violation of the principle of territorial integrity. The Committee called on Britain to make the territory whole. Britain ignored this too. In December 1967, the General Assembly adopted a third resolution criticising the detachment of Chagos. That too was ignored.

The following spring, Mauritius became an independent country, but with its territory incomplete. As the British flag came down and the Mauritian flag was raised, Governor Rennie, in a ceremonial hat adorned with many white feathers, offered a hand to Sir Seewoosagur Ramgoolam, the first Prime Minister of independent Mauritius. Watching a newsreel, I noticed that Sir Seewoosagur paused before accepting the hand of the outgoing Governor. The Governor's final act was to adopt a new constitution for Mauritius, one that comprised only "the territories which immediately before 12 March 1968 constituted the colony of Mauritius." The new definition excluded Chagos. A month later, Mauritius became the 125th member of the UN. In New York, Otis Redding was top of the charts with "Sittin' on the Dock of the Bay."

. . .

On Peros Banhos, Liseby and her family and friends were unaware of these developments. She knew not that she was now the inhabitant of a new British colony, rather than an independent Mauritius. She knew nothing about any agreement with the United States. And she did not know that her time on Peros Banhos would soon come to an end, that shortly she would be deported from the island and her home, along with everyone else.

Others did know what was coming. The British mission in New York worried about the "arguable thesis" that the detachment was illegal. The removal of the entire population would make matters far worse, "difficult to reconcile" with the "sacred trust" of Chapter XI of the UN Charter, and its Article 73. British officials faced a very human problem, so they decided to run with Lord Caradon's lie: they would tell the world that Chagos had no "permanent population."

Ever creative, the British asserted that Liseby Bertrand and all the Chagossians were merely "contract labourers," not inhabitants with families, many of whom had lived on the islands for generations, known as "Ilois." Liseby's ties to the island, passed down a long line of forebears, including the enslaved, were cast aside. We must be "very tough," the Foreign Office decided. "The object of the exercise is to get some rocks which will remain ours," an official noted, so Chagos becomes a place with "no indigenous population except seagulls." The fiction unlocked the British colonial imagination. "Along with the Birds go some few Tarzans or Men Fridays whose origins are obscure," wrote Mr. (later Lord) D.A. Greenhill. Soon they would be gone, removed to Mauritius and other distant places.

The forcible removal of hundreds of human beings was carried out in three phases, starting in 1967. The first to be removed were those who happened to be temporarily away from Chagos, in Mauritius or elsewhere. Sorry, they were told, but there is no boat available to return you to Chagos. The next to go, following a decision taken by Harold Wilson and Foreign Secretary Michael Stewart in April 1969, were those living on Diego Garcia. The island is now "closed," the inhabitants were informed. Some were transported to Peros Banhos or other islands; others were taken to Mauritius or the Seychelles. Years later, some who were deported arrived at London's Gatwick Airport, to make new lives in nearby Crawley. The final group to be removed included those who lived on all the other islands of Chagos, including Peros Banhos. A diaspora was created, one for which the British were fully responsible, for the agreement with the United States "required only Diego Garcia to be empty," the British High Commissioner in Port Louis was later told. "They had no objections to the other Chagos Islands remaining populated; it was our decision to clear the lot and resettle in Mauritius."

By the summer of 1973, the entire population of Chagos had been forcibly removed, about 1,500 people. They left behind homes and possessions, furnishings and animals, and many dogs. The pets created another problem, a solution for which was found with bullets and strychnine. When this solution failed, the dogs were rounded up, locked into a copra-drying shed, gassed, then incinerated.

None of this was reported in the British press. At the time I was a schoolboy, taking lessons in history but unaware of such matters. My school classes offered a very different account of British colonialism, as my history book from 1973, which I still have, reminded me, with its wistful chapter on "Sunset on the Empires." On India we were taught that Lord Mountbatten, Britain's last viceroy, was "a remarkable man," one who compared favourably to Mahatma Gandhi, a "wizened, bony, almost monkey-like" leader with "cheap spectacles, a vegetarian, a pacifist." I was taught that the end of empire was akin to the situation of "parent and child," where the parent won't admit that the child is quite grown up, and the child rebelliously insists that it is. "The child usually gets its way in the end, and learns, sometimes painfully, by its own mistakes."

LISEBY, 1973

Liseby Bertrand has no memory of the independence of Mauritius, because it never reached Peros Banhos, or any part of Chagos. She was fifteen, working as a nanny. "I was looking after the two children of Monsieur Jean Guillemet, the new administrator of Chagos," she recalled. "His daughter Gilberte was also born on Peros Banhos. Today she lives in Port Louis, we are still in touch."

It was only after independence and dismemberment, living on the newly created colony of "BIOT," that she first encountered an English person. "Maybe it was in 1970 or 1971, after the British bought the Agalega Company. A man who was called 'the Administrator' visited Peros Banhos, I think his name was Mr. Todd. That was the first time I saw a white person on Peros Banhos. Actually, it was the first time I saw any white person." (Her recollection was accurate: John Rawling Todd, who joined the Colonial Service in 1955 and served as Administrator of the British Indian Ocean Territory from 1965 to 1974, ruled from the Seychelles and only rarely visited.)

Around the time of Mr. Todd's visit to Peros Banhos, whispers began to circulate. "We started to hear rumours that we would have to leave the islands, all of us who lived there. I didn't really believe it. That was the moment when I understood there was a difference between white people and Black people. We were going to leave because we were Black. We understood that."

In 1972, on Peros Banhos, Liseby married her childhood sweetheart, France Elysé, who was also from the island. "Our wedding was on 11 December, a day I remember very well. The marriage ceremony was conducted by the administrator. I remember the dress I wore, and the party in the 'Salle Verte,' the green room. We danced and danced. I became Madame Elysé."

Did she have a photograph of that special day? "No, I have no photo of my wedding. You know what? I have no photo of my entire childhood. The first photograph of me was taken only when I was twenty years old, after we left Peros Banhos."

Her husband worked as a blacksmith in the forge of the Agalega Company. "After the wedding, I stopped living in my father's house and moved in with my husband, to the house he shared with his mother, my mother-in-law. My husband's sister is the mother of Olivier Bancoult, who is the lawyer for the Chagossians. I am his aunt."

Within a year, she was pregnant with their first child. Before the birth, however, the rumours became fact: the inhabitants of Peros Banhos were informed that their island was to be "closed," that they would all have to leave. Liseby was on the last boat to depart the islands and Chagos, one of a group of about 400 to be forcibly removed.

"The twenty-seventh of April 1973, that was the day we all left. Me. My husband. My father. My brothers and sisters. I was nearly twenty years old. I was pregnant."

They were not allowed to take much with them on the journey. "They told us to leave everything behind. We were not allowed to take our dogs. Each of us was allowed one trunk, which we filled with our most important items. We didn't have a suitcase, we had wooden *malles*, trunks. Maybe we were allowed 25 or 30 kilos each. I still have my trunk."

They gathered on the jetty, the one I knew from the old black and white photograph. One by one they made their way onto a boat, the MS *Nordvaer*, built in 1958, in Elmshorn, Germany. For years it sailed up and down the coast of Norway, between Trondheim and the Lofoten Islands, with a small number of passengers, genteel English tourists. It was purchased by the government of the "British Indian Ocean Territory," and one day, many years later, it was run aground in the Seychelles, on Desnoeufs Island, to serve as a breakwater.

The boat's English passengers were replaced by Chagossians. "The conditions were not good," Liseby recalled. "The journey across the ocean took four days. We arrived in Mauritius on 2 May 1973. We were sad. It felt like they treated us like animals, or slaves." On arrival, the passengers initially refused to disembark, with nowhere to go, and no money or accommodation available. "No one from the government of Mauritius was there to meet them, or from the Catholic church," I was told by a Chagossian living in Crawley, "and the boat's captain, Ronny Saminaden, said he had never transported people in such terrible conditions." These dreadful circumstances would leave a lasting legacy, one that would cause many Chagossians to question whether Mauritius could be relied upon to look after their interests in the future. It would fuel disagreements among the diaspora on how best to protect their interests, and give effect to their will.

France and Liseby Elysé, Port Louis, Mauritius, 1974.

Eventually, the government of Mauritius provided Liseby and her husband, France, with basic accommodation near the harbour at Port Louis, an area called Baie du Tombeau. "Soon after we arrived I lost the child, my first," Liseby said. "I suppose it was the trauma and the sadness." Around this time, Liseby and France were photographed for the first time, with an anxious air.

"The building we lived in was large, with three floors, each divided into apartments. I think they were built for dock workers. One or two blocks were empty, that is where they put us, the Chagossians. The conditions were not desirable. There were no windows, no doors, there was debris and rubbish all around. We cleaned the place up, and that was where we lived, for fourteen years, until 1987. There were four or five of us in each room."

Liseby started to work almost immediately. "I had to, as we needed money. We had nothing. I began in a shop; later I worked as a maid. Soon I was pregnant again. My first child was born there, in 1977, a boy. We named him Desiré. He died in 2016, in England. After him I had five more children, a girl we named Anesa, and then four more boys. Jimmy. Ivan. Brian. Andy."

Three of the boys now live in Manchester, England, and the other son and daughter live in Mauritius. "They all want to go back to Peros Banhos," she added. "So do my brothers and sisters. All of them are alive, although two live in England, in Crawley, France and Toto. Each of us thought about Peros Banhos, every day. We all wondered what became of it. We still do, every day."

PART THREE

1984

"[T]he pauperisation and expulsion of the weak in the interests of the powerful still gives little to be proud of."

—LORD JUSTICE STEPHEN SEDLEY, London, 2004

My first contact with the world of international law was in the autumn of 1980, as a nineteen-year-old university student. My teacher was Professor Jennings, a pragmatic Yorkshireman with a dry sense of humour and bushy eyebrows. Soon to become a judge at the International Court in The Hague, he catalysed my interest in a subject that seemed more closely connected to my own family situation, as my mother had been a child refugee. I still have my lecture notes from that year, a course I recall with much happiness, 300 students crammed into a grand lecture hall. The notes confirm that colonialism and self-determination were not addressed, although there was a passing reference to the Court's 1966 South West Africa judgement and the limits of the judicial function, but with no mention of the case's controversy or racial elements. My class was almost entirely white.

I stayed on for an extra year to take a graduate degree in international law, which became my life. My teachers introduced me to new topics: Mr. Lauterpacht, the only child of Sir Hersch, lectured on the new law of the sea, and Mr. Greenwood taught us about the laws of war. One of his classes gave rise to a spirited debate on the legality of the use of nuclear weapons, in which he and I expressed sharply opposing views, although this did not cause him to mark me down in the final exam, a fact much appreciated then and now. It was the lectures given by Mr. Allott, however, that opened new vistas, explicitly raising the connection between law and politics and history, even if Britain's colonial past did not feature prominently. My initial education in international law, which I look back on with much happiness, was dominated by teachers who were male and white, schooled in a view of the world in which Britain was presented as special, a rare player with an abiding commitment to the rule of law.

The following year, 1983, was spent in the United States, where the interplay between politics and law was embraced more fully. I worked as a research assistant to Professor David Kennedy at Harvard Law School, encountering a world in which many of the students were not white. For the first time I attended an international law class taught by a Black professor, Clyde Ferguson, who contributed to the drafting of a 1967 UNESCO declaration on race and racial prejudice, with an accent on colonialism, slavery and racism. His course on human rights offered a very different perspective from the one I was used to.

In the spring of 1984, I was living in a small apartment on Massachusetts Avenue, near Harvard Square. Each day I bought a newspaper at the Out of Town News kiosk, and to this day recall the morning I saw a front-page headline in the *New York Times*, one that seemed to connect with my world: "Nicaragua Takes Case Against the U.S. to World Court."

The article described the efforts of the small central American country to obtain a ruling from the Court that the United States was illegally mining Nicaragua's harbours, and supporting other attacks. It referenced Nicaragua's lawyers, Professor Abram Chayes, from Harvard, and Professor Ian Brownlie, from Oxford. The US State Department hoped the Court would decline to exercise jurisdiction, as it had done in the South West Africa cases. Professor Chayes, who had been President John F. Kennedy's legal adviser at the State Department during the Cuban Missile Crisis, characterised this as "a nit-picking lawyer's argument."

The article did not set out the full story behind the case, which I only learned about many years later. It was the product of creative lawyering, involving two relatively junior lawyers, Judith Appelbaum and Paul Reichler, who worked for a law firm in Washington,

DC, that was hired by the new Sandinista government of Nicaragua, and a Nicaraguan lawyer, Carlos Arguello. Initially, the aim was to recover moneys spirited out of the country by its former dictator, Anastasio Somoza, he who had warmly received Sir Percy and Lady Spender. Following the election of President Ronald Reagan, Reichler and Appelbaum joined another firm which, after the US invasion of Grenada in October 1983, balked at the prospect of suing the United States in The Hague ("not in the scope of the work we wanted to be doing for Nicaragua"). The two established their own firm, Reichler & Appelbaum, working with Carlos Arguello.

On 9 April 1984, Nicaragua filed a case at the Court. Those who drafted the application did not foresee that it would allow the Court to repair the damage done by the South West Africa judgements. It would also open another door through which, many years later, Madame Elysé would pass.

CAMP JUSTICE

To understand the confluence of events that allowed the Court to become an agent for change, it is necessary to go back a little further in time. For a student of international law who came of age in the 1980s, as I did, the past was a different country. Unlike today's immediate access thanks to the internet, a document from the UN in New York or from the Court in The Hague would take months to reach the university library. Information about major developments, like Nicaragua's case at the Court, or the signature of the landmark convention on the law of the sea two years earlier, was not easy to obtain. Information about more modest political developments, like the speech Mauritian Prime Minister Aneerood Jugnauth gave at the UN in the autumn of 1982, which first articulated the country's claim to Chagos, would not reach us at all. The speech might have made waves in Port Louis, but in Britain no one would have noticed, except perhaps for a few folk in the Foreign Office.

I knew nothing of Chagos back then, just as I knew nothing of

Bob Hope and the "American Beauties," Diego Garcia, 1971.

the Falklands, or Las Malvinas, forcibly occupied by Argentina in April 1982, which claimed the islands as its own. We knew nothing of a US military base at Diego Garcia, created eleven years earlier, in March 1971, on an island from which the inhabitants had been forcibly removed. "Absolutely must go," US Navy Admiral Elmo Zumwalt had declared of the entire population. "Project Reindeer Station," as the US naval communication facility was initially called, started with a short landing strip for aircraft. The following year, the station was renamed "Camp Justice," without irony, with the runway extended to accommodate giant C-141 transport planes.

The first aircraft to land, on Christmas Day, discharged Mr. Bob Hope, the famous entertainer, along with a troupe of seventy-five performers, including thirty-two "American Beauties" and an Australian recently crowned as Miss World. Framed by pristine waters and palm trees, the performers sang and danced and cracked jokes, entertaining the troops in a manner that seemed oblivious to the island's history, a plantation worked by enslaved people whose descendants had just been forcibly deported.

In August 1973, a Taiwanese company constructed a ship canal in Diego Garcia's deep lagoon, with a turning basin for larger military vessels. The runway was extended once more, with taxiways and a parking apron added, along with hangars and other facilities. A minor "communications" facility became a major military base, authorised by the US Congress to offer support for military operations across the Indian Ocean. The *Washington Post* ran a story about the abject conditions in which many of the Chagossians now found themselves, and their petition for better lives, but this made no headway. Nor did a report by the Minority Rights Group in London, contrasting Diego Garcia with the Falklands. With the overthrow of the Shah of Iran by an Islamic revolution and Soviet troops entering Afghanistan, at the end of the 1970s, the region became a focal point for new Cold War and other geopolitical struggles. Diego Garcia became ever more important to the United States as more than half a billion dollars were invested over the next decade, expanding the base to host rapid deployment forces and a large fleet of naval vessels.

· · ·

As "Camp Justice" and the deportations were underway, the Court in The Hague grappled with the fallout from the South West Africa cases. The 1966 judgements caused many countries recently emerged from colonial rule to view the Court with scepticism, a relic of the colonial era. Few cases reached the Court, and those that did came from Europe. A maritime dispute between West Germany, Denmark and the Netherlands was the only contentious matter to go before the Court in the immediate years that followed.

Four years after the 1966 judgements, however, a first crack did appear. The Security Council had ordered South Africa to withdraw from Namibia, determining that its continued occupation was illegal and the mistreatment of the inhabitants a flagrant violation of human rights. The Security Council instructed countries to have no dealings with South Africa in relation to Namibia. When South Africa refused to leave, the Council requested an advisory opinion from the Court, on the legal consequences of South Africa's intransigence.

The composition of the Court had changed: Sir Percy Spender had retired and his nemesis, Sir Zafarullah Khan, was now the President. In June 1971, by a large majority—with Gerald Fitzmaurice dissenting—the Court ruled that South Africa's presence in Namibia was illegal, that it must withdraw "immediately," and that all members of the UN must avoid any act in support of the occupier.

The Court's decision drew on General Assembly resolutions, including 1514, which were considered to have "operative" effects, that is to say, to produce legally binding consequences. Another resolution, 2145, had terminated South Africa's mandate in Namibia and enlisted the cooperation of the Security Council to procure South Africa's withdrawal. By a large majority, the judges declared that the practice of apartheid—discriminating against people on the basis of race, colour and other factors—violated the fundamental human rights of Namibians and the purposes and principles of the UN Charter. South Africa was an outlaw state.

President Zafarullah Khan penned a strongly worded statement: continued colonial rule by South Africa was "a denial of self-determination as envisaged in the Charter." This was a direct rebuttal to Fitzmaurice's lengthy, irritated dissent, over a hundred pages of legal formalisms. South Africa should have been allowed to appoint an *ad hoc* judge, Fitzmaurice complained; Khan and two other judges should not have sat; and the case should have been rejected on the merits. While he respected the "humanitarian sentiments" of the opinion, Fitzmaurice wrote, he could not accept the reasoning: imbued with a continuing colonial instinct, he considered that South Africa had not violated its mandate, which could not be terminated by the General Assembly, and that resolution 2145 was invalid and without legal effect. (Reading him again today, I recall a dissent he wrote a few years later, as a judge at the European Court of Human Rights, in a case about the birching of a fifteen-year-old boy on the Isle of Man. The Court having ruled such actions to be degrading and illegal, he dissented, based on his belief that the "natural perversity" of young people meant they regarded corporal punishment handed out to them as "matters of pride and congratulation.")

By the 1970s, Fitzmaurice was an isolated voice. The International Court was about to embark on a new adventure, as the sense of a post-colonial world beckoned.

THE SEA

If the 1971 advisory opinion heralded a new tide, it did not immediately wash away the wariness of many developing countries, particularly in Africa, towards the Court. Concerns were articulated with ferocity in the negotiation of a new treaty, the UN Convention on the Law of the Sea, concluded in December 1982 with a signing ceremony in Montego Bay, Jamaica. The Convention took more than a decade to negotiate, with over 150 countries involved.

UNCLOS, as the Convention is known, was seen as an early post-colonial instrument, one that sought to give effect to the principle of self-determination. The law of the sea treaty addressed technical matters, like freedom on the high seas, the rights of the coastal state and the delimitation of sea boundaries. Yet it also developed new rules, giving coastal states the right to fish in an "exclusive economic zone" up to 200 miles from their coasts, and to exploit oil and gas on a continental shelf further out. It was also innovative, with new rules on the protection of the marine environment and on the "common heritage of mankind," giving all states, however poor or distant, and even those that had no access to the sea, rights over mineral resources under the seabed.

The new rules came with new institutions, and mechanisms

to resolve the future disputes that would surely arise, a matter on which the United States took the lead. Many countries wanted a new international tribunal, to avoid the Court in The Hague. The existing institutions served the "interests of colonialism," China and other countries believed, and new rules were needed to reflect new interests. Invoking resolution 1514, Namibia joined the Convention even though it was still illegally occupied by South Africa.

The negotiations on dispute settlement became a lever for change, with strong views expressed from around the globe. Trinidad & Tobago was one of the many countries with serious reservations about the Court, which was quiescent, and Cuba made clear it would not go to The Hague, to an institution that served the *status quo*. African countries expressed strong objections to the Court: Madagascar wanted a new court for law of the sea matters, as did Nigeria, although it could live with a residual role for The Hague. Mauritius proposed arbitration and *ad hoc* panels created for each dispute, rather than the Court. In the Americas, Ecuador wanted a new tribunal to reflect "the aspirations of developing countries," and Surinam proposed a tribunal with "a larger role for developing countries." From Asia, Bangladesh and Indonesia joined calls for a new court, as did Syria and the United Arab Emirates, to take account of the interests of developing countries. The momentum was broad and irresistible, as former colonies weighed in. Ireland expressed doubts about a new court, but recognised that with many countries lacking confidence in the Court, a new institution would have to be created.

And so it was. Part XV of the Convention created a choice for the settlement of maritime disputes: parties could submit a case to The Hague, or to a new International Tribunal for the Law of the Sea, or to arbitration. Twelve more years would pass before UNCLOS came into force, and when it did, the new Tribunal was established in Hamburg. It had twenty-one judges, six more than the Court in The Hague, with no guaranteed slots for judges from the five permanent members of the Security Council, unlike The Hague. First elected in 1996, a majority of the judges came from the developing world: the Tribunal's first President, Thomas Mensah of Ghana, was a child of colonialism, born under British rule in the Gold Coast colony. I appeared as counsel in the first case, in a barrister's wig and gown at a hearing in a makeshift courtroom in Hamburg's Town Hall; years later, Judge Mensah told me, with a big grin, that he wondered on that occasion whether the world of international justice would ever not be populated by a regular British presence.

The creation of the law of the sea Tribunal in Hamburg meant The Hague lost its monopoly. It now faced competition, as a marketplace of international courts came into being, a reflection, perhaps, of the ideologies of Margaret Thatcher and Ronald Reagan that came to dominate politics in some countries in the early 1980s. Competition in the arcane world of international law would come to be significant in the case of Chagos.

NICARAGUA

Two years after UNCLOS was signed, Nicaragua sued the United States in The Hague. It was a David and Goliath moment, one that gave the Court an opportunity to renew itself in the face of competition from Hamburg.

Nicaragua was a colony of Spain until it gained independence in the early nineteenth century. For many decades it was ruled by the Somozas, a despotic family with staunchly anti-communist and virulently pro-American views. In July 1979, after decades in power, the Somozas were toppled by the Frente Sandinista de Liberación Nacional, the Sandinistas. President Reagan imposed a US blockade on the country, offering money, training and arms to the Contrarrevolución, an anti-Sandinista paramilitary group known as the "Contras."

In the autumn of 1983, the main aim was to shift the focus

of debate in the US Congress, to influence a vote on aid to the Contras. Professor Chayes hoped the case would allow the United States to hold a mirror to itself, to challenge its self-image "as a law-abiding nation proud of its role in creating, supporting and defending the international legal order." Nicaragua's good fortune, Professor Chayes believed, was that the World Court was well-regarded in the US, having recently condemned Iran for seizing the American embassy and taking diplomats hostage in Tehran.

Faced with Soviet and Cuban opposition to the legal initiative, Nicaragua's lawyers prepared a memorandum on the Court, the judges, the arguments, the evidence and the likely reaction of the Americans, both legal and political. The exercise evolved over several months, involving "discreet consultations" with friendly governments, including Mexico, whose Foreign Minister would later be a judge on the Court. Many thought Nicaragua had a strong case. At a meeting in New York, the views of a serving judge at The Hague, from a non-aligned country, were sought. Would the Court render an impartial judgement, or would the judges feel obliged to favour the US? The answer that came back was "unequivocal," one that catalysed the decision to proceed: the composition of the Court meant that it could be counted upon to decide the case on its merits, the advisers were told.

In April 1984, Nicaragua filed a case against the United States, alleging violations of the prohibition on the use of force in the UN Charter and general international law. The US would argue that military force was being used lawfully, in collective self-defence, to support El Salvador against Nicaragua's incursions into its territory.

In May 1984, after a short hearing, under the presidency of Judge Elias of Nigeria, the Court ordered provisional measures, pending a full hearing of the case. The measures required the United States to end its blockade of Nicaraguan ports and the laying of mines, and to respect the sovereignty and political independence of Nicaragua. The order was widely reported in the press, renewing interest in the

Court across the developing world. A few months later, in November, the Court ruled by a large majority that it had jurisdiction to hear the case: the American judge, Stephen Schwebel, offered a solitary dissent, unsupported by his British colleague, Judge Jennings, my first teacher of international law. The US reaction was to announce that it would not participate further in the case, and distance itself from the Court. The State Department asserted that justice was being subverted, that Nicaragua and its Cuban and Soviet sponsors were using the Court "as a political weapon."

The case proceeded to the merits, raising questions about the circumstances in which one country could use force to intervene in the affairs of another. The case had no apparent connection with self-determination, yet the issue snuck in unexpectedly, prompted by an academic article with the title "Coercion and Self-Determination." Its author, Professor Reisman, argued for an expansive interpretation of the UN Charter, which limited the use of force to self-defence or where authorised by the Security Council. He argued for countries to be able to use military force to liberate the people of another country where "popular will" was usurped "without a base of popular support." The article made no mention of Nicaragua, yet its presence was palpable. Article 2(4) should be interpreted to "enhance" self-determination, the article argued, not limit it. If force could not be used to protect the basic rights of others—to promote self-determination—international law would be undermined, a consequence that would "rape common sense."

It was now the spring of 1985, and Judge Singh of India was President of the Court. This was around the time I first visited the institution, a young academic accompanying law students to a moot competition—a mock legal trial—at the Palace of Peace. I recall my first impression, from a distance, peering through high iron railings towards a grand building from another era, one that evoked impressions of authority and the power of the law as we would like it to be. I did not appreciate, back then, that over the years, as I returned, my feelings towards the place would evolve, with ups and downs.

In the summer of 1986, the Court gave judgement in the Nicaragua case. A large majority of the judges ruled that the United States had violated Nicaragua's rights under international law, and infringed its sovereignty. They rejected the US argument of collective self-defence, ruling that it owed reparations to Nicaragua. Judge Schwebel dissented, evoking the ideas of Professor Reisman in a spirited but solitary argument on self-determination. "In contemporary international law," he wrote, "the right of self-determination, freedom and independence of peoples is universally recognized," and those invoking the right should be able to obtain foreign assistance or support. If the US could offer moral, political and humanitarian assistance to a people struggling for self-determination, why not also offer arms, especially if the struggle was "in pursuance of [. . .] decolonization or against racial domination?" "What is a colony, and who is a colonizer, are the subjects of sharply differing views," he explained. The argument attracted no support, as other judges distanced themselves from the idea that the US could use force to liberate the "colonised" majority of Nicaragua's population.

In this way, the Nicaragua judgement kept the door firmly shut on expanding the use of self-determination in ways that Bunche and Boland would never have intended. At the same time, the ruling changed perceptions of the Court, cleansing many of the stains left by South West Africa. It helped the Court emerge from a wilderness, a first step to making it a place to which a former colony might turn, in future, to free itself from continued colonial domination.

MADAME ELYSÉ, 1984

The Court ruled that international law required the United States to pay reparation to Nicaragua. Following a change of government, however, and an offer of substantial economic assistance from the new administration of President George H.W. Bush, Nicaragua agreed to settle the case. The Court never determined the amount of damages to be paid. For Chagos, however, reparations continued to be a live issue.

In the 1970s, Britain paid £3 million (US $4.5 million) in compensation to Mauritius for "loss of sovereignty" over the islands. Four years later, a further £650,000 (US $975,000) was made available for the resettlement of "persons displaced." This was stated to be "in full and final discharge" of Britain's obligations. Modest in amount, some of the moneys made their way to the Chagossians.

"Were you paid compensation?" I asked Madame Elysé.

"A bit," she replied. "A little bit."

She recalled the details, set out in various documents.

"In 1978 I was paid 7,590 rupees." That was about £500 (US $750).

"In 1982 they gave me another 10,000 rupees." About £600 (US $900).

"In 1983 I got another 3,000 rupees." £200 (US $300).

In the decade following her forcible removal from Peros Banhos, she was paid the grand sum of £1,300 (US $1,950).

"In 1984 there was a bigger sum, about 36,900 rupees. That was held for me by the Mauritian Central Housing Authority. We used it, my husband and I, to build a house. In 1988 we moved into our new house, and we have lived there ever since."

On several occasions I have visited Madame Elysé and her family in this house, where they have now lived for three decades. She has prepared traditional Chagossian meals, with her husband and children, and a grandson who likes to wear a bright green "West Coast Chillin" T-shirt. With her friends, also from Chagos, we have sat together for hours at the long table on the porch, next to two fine murals painted by the artist Clément Siatous, who was also born on Peros Banhos. One shows the beach at Peros Banhos, a setting sun, birds and palm trees, fishermen, sailing boats. The other is of the administrator's house, with its white staircase leading to a balcony and entrance on the first floor.

Peros Banhos by Clément Siatous (c. 2000).

. . .

If the British hoped the meagre payments to Madame Elysé and other Chagossians might bring matters to an end, they would be disappointed. Over time, feelings of injustice tend to ferment, and channels must be found to direct the energies that are produced. Litigation is one such channel.

In the mid-1970s, Michel Vencatassen brought the first legal case in the English courts. Forcibly removed from Chagos, he sued the British government for "intimidation and deprivation of liberty." Fearing adverse publicity, the British government settled the case for £4 million (US $6 million), the moneys held on trust for the Chagossians. To obtain a payment, individuals were required to renounce their rights, by signing a slip of paper. Madame Elysé signed a slip, which read:

> In consideration of the compensation paid to me . . . I renounce to all claims, present or future, that I may have against the Government of the United Kingdom . . . their servants, agents or

contractors, in respect of . . . all acts, matters and things done by or pursuant to the British Indian Ocean Territory Order 1965, including the closure of the plantations in the Chagos Archipelago, my departure or removal from there, loss of employment . . .

Never having learned to write, Madame Elysé placed a single thumbprint on the paper. Not having learned to read, she told me she did not really know what the document said, nor that the act would cause her to forfeit so much. Many years later, a UN human rights body disparaged the validity of the document for these reasons.

Around the time Madame Elysé was placing her thumb on the paper, the British government was dispatching a naval force to the South Atlantic to recover the distant Falkland Islands/Malvinas from an unexpected Argentine occupation. To justify their actions, they invoked the right to self-determination and the UN Charter, to protect the 2,841 inhabitants of the British colony. The difference of approach to the treatment of the two populations—one white, the other Black—was not widely recognised. Thirty years later, in May 2015, the British government would even publish a paper titled "Falkland Islanders' Right to Self-Determination." It did so with a straight face, as it opposed the right of Mauritius to self-determination in relation to Chagos. One rule for whites, another for Blacks.

The settlement of the Vencatassen litigation did not end the story. Olivier Bancoult, the nephew of Madame Elysé, embarked on a lengthy series of legal actions before the English courts. Born on Peros Banhos, Olivier was four years old when he was deported to Mauritius with his family. After school, at the age of eighteen, he developed an interest in the legal rights of the Chagossians. "I wanted justice for my family and my people."

In 1998, Olivier Bancoult filed a first case at the High Court in London, to challenge a 1971 British immigration law that prevented Chagossians from returning to their homes. The case, Bancoult No. 1, was successful, as the High Court ruled that the law was unlawful. The power to legislate for "peace, order and good government," on which it was based, did not allow the permanent expulsion of the inhabitants, the High Court declared. The British government accepted the ruling, and Foreign Secretary Robin Cook announced that the Chagossians would be able to return to their homes on Peros Banhos and other outer islands. A new immigration ordinance was adopted, allowing entry and return to all parts of Chagos except Diego Garcia. After a quarter of a century, Madame Elysé could imagine a return to her homeland.

As they awaited developments, Olivier filed a second case at the High Court, Bancoult No. 2. This sought compensation and the restoration of the property rights of those forcibly removed, together with measures to allow them to return. The case failed and no appeal was allowed. The High Court recognised that families and communities had been wrecked, that British officials had acted in an "underhand" manner, but the claim was unsupported by the law.

Chagossian children protest, Port Louis, Mauritius, 2004.

In 2004 the British government abruptly changed direction on Madame Elysé's ability to return to her home. This followed Britain's decision to join the United States in removing Saddam Hussein from power and occupying Iraq, a decision presaged by the removal of Robin Cook as Foreign Secretary, and his replacement with Jack Straw. A new *British Indian Ocean Territory (Constitution) Order 2004* was adopted, to extinguish once more the ability of the Chagossians to return to Peros Banhos and other islands. This caused widespread protests in Port Louis. Four Chagossian children held a placard at one of the demonstrations, a moment caught by a photographer: "UK = Crime Against Humanity."

. . .

Olivier Bancoult returned to the High Court in London to challenge the 2004 Order. In Bancoult No. 3, the High Court ruled that the order was "irrational" and unlawful, as it failed to promote the interests of the Chagossians. On appeal, the Court of Appeal ruled that the removal and exclusion of the Chagossians was an abuse of the power of colonial governance, interfering with the Chagossians' "legitimate expectations" to be able to return to their home. Lord Justice Sedley, writing for the High Court, summarised the "shameful" treatment of the Chagossians: the "deliberate misrepresentation of the Ilois' history and status, designed to deflect any investigation by the United Nations; the use of legal powers designed for the governance of the islands for the illicit purpose of depopulating them; the uprooting of scores of families from the only way of life and means of subsistence that they knew; the want of anything like adequate provision for their resettlement." The "pauperisation and expulsion of the weak in the interests of the powerful still gives little to be proud of."

The government appealed to the House of Lords, the highest court in the land, where it won by a narrow majority. The measures were not "irrational," three of the five judges ruled, as matters of this kind were to be decided by the executive, not the courts. "[T]he right of abode is a creature of the law," wrote Lord Hoffmann for the majority, and "the law gives it and the law may take it away." Yes, the removal and resettlement of the Chagossians was carried out with "a callous disregard of their interests," and the argument that a return of the Chagossians to Peros Banhos and the outer islands would threaten national security was "fanciful speculation." But no, the interests of the Chagossians could not prevail: Her Majesty in Council was "entitled to legislate for a colony in the interests of the United Kingdom," and "required to take into account the interests of the colony," but in the event of a conflict between those interests she was "entitled, on the advice of Her United Kingdom ministers, to prefer the interests of the United Kingdom."

Lord Bingham wrote a strong dissent, concluding that the 2004 Order was irrational. The base at Diego Garcia did not extend to the outer islands, and resettlement did not threaten it or national security. Letters written by American officials to strengthen the British government's hand in the litigation were "highly imaginative" but offered "no credible reason" to support security concerns. Bingham noted that in the 1960s, US officials had made clear they had no objection to the Chagossians remaining on the outer islands.

The case went to the European Court of Human Rights in Strasbourg, established in 1950 as ideas about self-determination and human rights came to fruition. The European Court rejected the Chagossian claims, on the grounds that the applicants had been paid compensation and, in accepting it, renounced further claims. The conclusion was premised on the view that Britain's occupation of Chagos was lawful under international law.

The cases in London and Strasbourg, and a US court ruling that Chagossian claims raised "non justiciable political" matters of US foreign policy, extinguished Madame Elysé's hopes. Three decades after being forcibly removed from Peros Banhos, she felt "sad and depleted."

SEPTEMBER 11TH

As the brutal twentieth century came to a close, other developments were underway. Disparate, unexpected and apparently unrelated to the decolonisation of Mauritius, these developments would forge a path that led Madame Elysé to The Hague, and led to the question with which I opened this story.

As the Nicaragua case came to a close, South Africa's new President, F.W. de Klerk, took steps to dismantle apartheid, end the ban on the African National Congress, and release Nelson Mandela from twenty-seven years of imprisonment. South Africa finally departed the territory formerly known as South West Africa, a quarter of a century after the ruling by the International Court of Justice. Namibia celebrated its independence and joined the UN, the 159th member. At the inauguration of the country's first President, Nelson Mandela proclaimed a hope of an "inalienable right to human dignity" for all.

Across the ocean, in Rio de Janeiro in June 1992, government leaders signed a raft of agreements to protect the global environment. They included a little-noticed call for coastal states to conserve the biological diversity of the oceans. In time, the parties to the Convention on Biological Diversity would create marine protected areas, spaces in which human activity would be curtailed to conserve marine biodiversity.

In New York, after the collapse of the Soviet Union in December 1991, the instinct for justice that gave rise to the Nuremberg trials was momentarily rekindled. The Security Council created the first new international criminal tribunals in half a century, a response to terrible crimes committed in the former Yugoslavia and Rwanda. The list of "crimes against humanity" once more included deportation, the forcible displacement of civilians.

In Rome, in the summer of 1998, many countries created an International Criminal Court, five decades after Nuremberg. Article 7 of its Statute gave the ICC jurisdiction over the "crime against humanity" of "deportation or forcible transfer of population." I was in Rome that summer, on the delegation of the Solomon Islands, a small Pacific island country, working with a colleague on the drafting of the Statute's preamble. Left to our own instincts, we introduced into the text "the duty of every State to exercise its criminal jurisdiction over those responsible for international crimes." This was unprecedented, and we expected the line to be removed, but somehow it remained.

I was present as a consequence of a case I had argued for the Solomon Islands two years earlier, at the International Court, on the legality of the use of nuclear weapons. This followed a request for an advisory opinion, an unhappy question the response to which by the Court left open the possibility that nuclear weapons might lawfully be used in an exceptional circumstance. Yet the Court also recognised—for the first time—that the protection of the environment was now part of the corpus of international law. This was my first case at the Court, a lesson in legal *realpolitik* that came with an environmental silver lining. There was a moment in the proceedings that I have never quite managed to get out of my mind: as counsel for Samoa expressed "outrage" at the recent resumption of French nuclear testing in the South Pacific, several of us present in the Great Hall of Justice observed the French judge remove the headphones from his ears and place them before him on the table.

As these developments unfolded and converged, decolonisation proceeded, Eritrea and South Sudan joined the UN, to bring African membership to fifty-four countries, the largest group. Yet the continent was still colonised: Spain retained a couple of enclaves, two islands were under French rule, and Britain held on to the last colony it created in Africa—or anywhere in the world—the "British Indian Ocean Territory," stamped over Chagos.

Madame Elysé and the Chagossians had not given up. The protests continued, and on one occasion the British High Commissioner in Port Louis had to be secretly smuggled out of his own building. "In 2001 I had a fifteen-day demonstration against me," Mr. Snoxell reported, 300 Chagossians camped outside the High Commission. Personally supportive of change, the High Commissioner's efforts were firmly resisted by civil servants in London, taking refuge in the supposed intransigence of Washington. British officials merely "ventriloquised" the answers from the Americans, the former High Commissioner reported, transforming them into the sentiments they wanted. The reason was simple: the military base on Chagos had assumed an even greater significance.

In September 2001, nineteen men associated with Al Qaeda hijacked several planes and flew them into the World Trade Center in New York and the Pentagon, just outside Washington, DC. I was in New York that morning, teaching a course on international law as the Twin Towers fell. The US response, supported by Britain, was swift: military attacks on Afghanistan, a decision to remove Saddam Hussein from power in Iraq, and an extensive programme to apprehend suspected terrorists and render them to places of detention, interrogation and—by waterboarding and other means—torture.

Secretly, the United States deployed Diego Garcia as a part of this programme, with detainees passing through the old "Camp Justice" to other places of interrogation around the world. The British government denied the rumours, but in due course Foreign Secretary David Miliband was forced to apologise to Parliament for erroneous denials offered by his predecessor, Mr. Straw, and former Prime Minister Tony Blair. "Contrary to earlier explicit assurances that Diego Garcia had not been used for rendition flights, recent US investigations have now revealed two occasions, both in 2002, when this had in fact occurred."

The US claimed that no detainee ever left a plane, and that no one was held or interrogated on Chagos. Over time this was contradicted by reliable military and intelligence sources in the United States, asserting that several detainees did spend time on the British colonial soil. In 2015 a senior State Department official confirmed that Diego Garcia was used by the CIA as a "transit site," to house people temporarily, where they were "interrogated from time to time." What did the British know? This was unclear, it being reported that British officials systematically destroyed flight logs in and out of Diego Garcia.

The Foreign Affairs Committee of the UK Parliament deplored

the failure of British oversight of its colony. The US Senate Select Committee on Intelligence reported that the CIA may have established a secret "black site" detention and interrogation facility for "high-value suspects" on Diego Garcia, which may have occurred with "full cooperation" from the British government.

. . .

Coincidentally, it was during this time that Mauritius redoubled its effort to recover Chagos, as Ton Vié released a song, "Peros Vert," that described the displacement of the Chagossians and would become something of an anthem. International litigation began to be explored, and the government retained the services of Professor Brownlie, who had successfully argued Nicaragua's case in The Hague. He prepared a lengthy memorandum on legal options, premised on his view that the detachment of Chagos from Mauritius was illegal, having violated resolution 1514 and the rules of international law on self-determination and territorial integrity.

Professor Brownlie identified two legal options. Mauritius could seek to persuade the General Assembly to request an advisory opinion from the Court, as the Assembly had done in relation to Namibia. This would be treacherous, however, since it would require a vote supported by a majority of members, and it could be expected that Britain and the United States would lobby hard to prevent such a vote. (Around this time, the Court gave an advisory opinion on Israel's construction of a wall that, it concluded, breached the right of self-determination of the Palestinian people: the ruling left open, however, the question of whether the right to self-determination was already a part of international law by the 1960s.)

A second possibility would be for Mauritius to sue Britain directly at the Court in a contentious case, following the path taken by Nicaragua. However, this option faced an obstacle, as Britain's acceptance of the Court's jurisdiction excluded disputes with countries that were members of the Commonwealth, like Mauritius. "You could leave the Commonwealth," Professor Brownlie suggested, and avoid the narrowly drafted terms of the jurisdictional limitation, which did not exclude cases with *former* members of the Commonwealth. The confidential advice leaked into the public domain. "Mauritius envisages leaving the Commonwealth," reported a newspaper in Port Louis. The article made its way to London, prompting the Foreign Office to amend Britain's acceptance of the Court's jurisdiction, to exclude any dispute with a *former* member of the Commonwealth. Introduced around the time of the 2004 Order to prevent Chagossians from returning, the amendment extinguished the possibility that Mauritius could leave the Commonwealth and bring a case against Britain. "The Government have acted to prevent such a move," a British minister told Parliament, without mention of Mauritius, Chagos or the "British Indian Ocean Territory."

The amendment closed the route taken by Nicaragua. The Palace of Peace seemed to be off the list of plausible options. And then Iraq happened.

PART FOUR

⬥

2003

"Unfortunately, along with the Birds go some few Tarzans or Men Fridays . . ."

—UK DIPLOMATIC CABLE, August 1966

On 20 March 2003 the United States and Britain went to war with Iraq, ostensibly to rid the country of "weapons of mass destruction" it turned out not to have. Many of the planes that launched the initial attack were B-1, B-2 and B-52 bombers flown from Diego Garcia. The fact was not widely known in Britain.

A week after war began, the Security Council met in New York. Most of the fifteen members, including Mauritius, believed that the Council had not authorised the use of force, by its resolution 1441—adopted the previous November—or by other means, which meant the use of force was illegal. Jagdish Koonjul, the permanent representative of Mauritius, told the Council that military action against Iraq required the authorisation of the Council, and intimated that no such authorisation was obtained, although he did not say this explicitly. The government of Mauritius did not wish to undermine the United States.

Six months later, in October 2003, *The Times* of London ran a piece by a leading British academic, with the headline: "Britain's War on Saddam Had the Law on Its Side." The article asserted that the war was lawfully based on Security Council resolution 678, adopted in 1990, as revived by later resolution 1441. According to the article, the failure to find weapons of mass destruction did not undermine the legality of the enterprise (unlike Suez, back in 1956, which had "no semblance of legality"). A small black and white photograph showed the author with a wistful smile, Christopher Greenwood, professor at the London School of Economics, barrister, my former teacher. The by-line added that Professor Greenwood "assisted the Government on the Iraq conflict."

Members of the English Bar tend not to write about matters in which they have been involved, at least not without the agreement of the client. The article—together with its timing—offered support for the British government's beleaguered effort to justify its actions in law.

It was this article that prompted me to explore the exact circumstances in which the British Attorney General, Lord Goldsmith, informed the Cabinet and Parliament that the war was lawful, supposedly authorised by resolution 1441. He did this on 17 March 2003, just three days before the war was launched. The Attorney General's statement was immediately controversial, yet it persuaded the Cabinet and Parliament to vote for war.

Digging deeper, I was shown a secret advice written ten days earlier by Lord Goldsmith for Prime Minister Tony Blair. Dated 7 March, the document was not shared with the Cabinet or Parliament, and contradicted the view expressed on 17 March. The "safest legal course," Lord Goldsmith advised in the unpublished document, would be to secure the adoption of a further resolution by the Security Council to authorise the use of force. Contrary to the article in *The Times*, Mr. Blair was explicitly warned by the Attorney General that the Security Council may not have authorised the use of force, that a court "might well conclude" that another, explicit resolution was necessary.

The disconnect between the two documents—the secret advice of 7 March, and the public statement of 17 March—was troubling. In due course, Parliament inquired as to the circumstances in which the latter statement was prepared. Lord Goldsmith declared he wrote it, assisted by "the Solicitor General, two officials in my office, three officials from the Foreign and Commonwealth Office, and Christopher Greenwood QC." How many lawyers does it take to prepare an opinion, it might be asked, and what, if any, was the connection with Chagos? I knew that the parliamentary statement allowed Britain to join the war, but did not know that it also authorised, in effect, the use of Diego Garcia: combat operations such as Iraq, I learned, were treated as an "extraordinary use" of the military base, going beyond routine activity, requiring explicit prior approval by the British government. The statement of 17 March 2003, and the authorisation that followed, it seemed, offered the necessary approval.

In this way, whether knowingly or not, Lord Goldsmith and his assistants allowed the territory of Chagos to be used to wage a war. It was this material that prompted me to write a book, *Lawless World*, which addressed the legal issues of the Iraq war, and was published in 2005. And it was this material, with its chapters on Iraq, prompted by an article in *The Times*, that caused me to be hired by the government of Mauritius to litigate the Chagos matter.

Every act, and every written word, is capable of having consequences, however unexpected or unintended.

MADAME ELYSÉ, 2006

Living in Port Louis, Madame Elysé was unaware that the land of her home was used to wage the war in Iraq. Her desire to return to Peros Banhos was undimmed, and three years after the war, the sentiments of the Chagossian community reached London. The British government decided the time was ripe to do something for those who had been forcibly removed. It settled on what would be referred to—quaintly to some, offensively to others—as "heritage visits."

Early in 2006, Madame Elysé learned of the possibility of a visit. She was in her mid-fifties, working as a maid for a Chinese-Mauritian family. Her father had passed away a few years earlier, still hoping to see Peros Banhos. "It never happened," Madame Elysé recalled, "so it became my dream, for him and for all of us." She was not alone. "My brothers, even the ones in England. My sister. My children. Everyone wanted to go." When the British offered a visit, she felt unable to resist the offer.

"We were a group of one hundred Chagossians on the journey,

we spent eight days together. It was March. We travelled with two priests, a Catholic, Gerard Monjeland, and an Anglican. We sailed from Port Louis just before Easter, a journey of four days to get there. We brought palm leaves, and on Palm Sunday we held a service on board. As the boat slowed down, we paid homage to those who were lost back in 1973, the ones who jumped into the sea or died before they reached Mauritius. I think there were nine of them, the ones who didn't live to see Mauritius. Some jumped, two were buried on the island of Rodrigues."

She described the visit with a clear, pained memory.

"First we arrived on Salomon island, for a very short visit, just a few hours. From there we took the boat to Peros Banhos. It was a Tuesday, maybe 4 April.

"We were allowed to be on Peros Banhos for just a few hours; then the British said we had to leave. No one was living there. We treated the visit as a pilgrimage, a time to honour our forebears. We

Nelson Mandela with Olivier Bancoult, South Africa (undated, 2000s).

wanted to tidy the place up, so we asked for equipment. We cleaned the church, the cemetery, the graves. I remember, we cleaned the grave of my father-in-law, Olivier Elysé."

Her nephew, Olivier Bancoult, was also on that trip, in search of his grandfather's grave. "The graves of the French staff, the administrators, had names, but not the Chagossians." He hoped to return with Liseby's husband, France, he explained. "He can show me where my grandfather is buried."

Liseby offered a graphic account of what she saw. "Everything was overgrown, totally abandoned. It was difficult to see our beautiful church in such a bad state, in disrepair, abandoned. There were coconut trees growing inside; the roof was gone. We cleaned up as best we could, and then we celebrated a mass, inside the church."

Liseby often recalled the celebration of that mass, how it left a deep impression, a sense of connection and community. "Someone filmed it. I have seen a film of that, of us singing. It was a powerful moment. We sang together, our song, it is called 'Peros Vert.'" She took up the words for me, in Creole, a gentle lilt that lifted the spirits, a hopeful song:

> *"Peros vert, peros vert, so pep noir, nu pep noir, nu pep noir, noune déraciné.*
> *zoizo crié, lisien zaper, mone perdi mo zil,*
> *goodbye, peros vert, goodbye, salomon, goodbye, diego,*
> *ki zamais mo pu trouve zot, mo lile, mo lile."*

Later I found a translation, and Olivier Bancoult sent me a video:

> *"Green Peros, we people are black, we who have been uprooted.*
> *The birds cry, the dogs bark, we who have lost our island,*
> *goodbye, Green Peros, goodbye, Salomon, goodbye, Diego,*
> *I will never see you, my island, my island."*

"I was very emotional on that visit," Liseby told me. "I should never have left. I should not have allowed our church to fall into such a state. I should not have abandoned the graves. I could not bear what I saw. I felt anger with the English, especially when I found what was left of my parents' home, just the concrete floor. We found it, I saw it."

The former inhabitants were allowed to spend a few hours on Peros Banhos, then shepherded back to the boat, which took a full day to reach Diego Garcia, 143 miles away. The group visited the old cemetery, to clean it up. "Like the one in Peros, it was overgrown." Later, as they headed back to the boat, they were surprised to come across another burial ground, a new one.

"We came to another cemetery, one that was run by the American military. It was very well tended, neat and clean, especially compared to our abandoned cemetery, where our families were buried. Then we saw that the cemetery was for their dogs. I have photos. It made me sad. It made me angry."

Madame Elysé fixed a stare, her face displaying a rare sense of anger, and of resistance, and of immense sadness.

"Where was the justice?" she asked. "Where *is* the justice?"

. . .

Justice takes its time as it wanders the UN corridors, as one body after another addressed the plight of the Chagossians.

A Working Group on Minorities raised concerns about the social and economic difficulties in Mauritius. They were ignored by Britain.

The Human Rights Committee recommended that Britain "should ensure that the Chagos islanders can exercise their right to return to their territory." Also ignored.

The Committee on the Elimination of Racial Discrimination recommended that discriminatory restrictions which prevented the Chagossians from entering Diego Garcia or other islands be withdrawn. Ignored.

Not long after Madame Elysé visited Peros Banhos, the Franco-Mauritian writer Jean-Marie Le Clézio wrote a public letter to President Barack Obama. You have "the power to change the fate of this people who came from east Africa in the age of slavery," the power to allow them to return to their native land, to honour their forebears, an act of justice, not of charity. He invited the leader of the free world to listen to the voice of Charlesia Alexis, to hear her sega song, to imagine what it meant to feel the misery of exile, and the hope of return.

I do not know whether President Obama received the letter or read it. I do know, however, that Monsieur Le Clézio did not receive a response.

MEN FRIDAYS

Le Clézio's letter was followed by a confluence of occurrences. It was the spring of 2010 when an unlikely interplay of the law of the sea convention, marine protected areas, the "war on terror" and the invasion of Iraq came together to cause British Foreign Secretary David Miliband to announce the creation of a vast Marine Protected Area around Chagos. The project, referred to as "the MPA," was intended to protect marine biodiversity, burnish Britain's green credentials, and cast a favourable light on Chagos, a distraction from its reported use for torture and war in Iraq.

Mr. Miliband announced that the MPA would cover a quarter of a million square miles, across which fishing and other activities would be prohibited. The initiative would double the world's coverage of protected oceans and demonstrate that "the UK takes its international environmental responsibilities seriously." Naturally, he made clear, the protected area would exclude the US base at Diego Garcia. Leading conservation groups, including the Pew Environment Group and the Zoological Society of London, hailed the proposal, as would, in due course, the less well-known Chagos Conservation Trust and the Bertarelli Foundation. A "historic victory for global ocean conservation," the NGOs believed. They remained conspicuously silent, however, about the impact on the Chagossians, who were disturbed by the announcement.

So was the government of Mauritius. Mr. Miliband's announcement caused it to reach out to lawyers, and I was invited to speak with Prime Minister Navi Ramgoolam. Port Louis had not been consulted, he explained, and invited us to find a way to challenge the lawfulness of the proposed MPA. He had a personal interest, as his father had negotiated the independence of Mauritius in 1965, which became effective in 1968. Mr. Ramgoolam told us that the British Prime Minister, Gordon Brown, had personally assured him just a few months earlier, in the margins of a meeting of the Commonwealth Heads of Government, that a marine protected area would not be created.

Mr. Ramgoolam instructed us to advise on the legality of the proposed MPA, and to identify avenues for redress. His request followed the sudden death of Professor Brownlie, who had advised Mauritius for many years, in a car accident in Egypt. "I have come to you because of your book on Iraq," he explained. "I want a lawyer who is comfortable taking on the British government."

Knowing little about Chagos, I read up about it, appalled by a story of continuing injustice and my own ignorance. I was well aware of Britain's colonial past, but not the story of the last colony it created in Africa. I accepted the instruction, and with the lawyers in Port Louis put together an experienced team. It included the lawyer Paul Reichler (an architect of the Nicaragua case), James Crawford (an Australian scholar widely recognised as the world's leading international litigator), and Elizabeth Wilmshurst (who had resigned as deputy legal adviser at the Foreign Office over the Iraq war). An outstanding group of younger lawyers was gathered in London, Washington and Boston, to work with Port Louis.

We were asked to identify options, relying on Professor Brownlie's groundwork. As a member of the Commonwealth, Mauritius could not bring a case directly against Britain to the Court in The Hague. The South West Africa route offered one possibility: to seek to persuade the UN General Assembly to request an advisory opinion from the Court, on the decolonisation of Mauritius and the illegality of the detachment of Chagos. The challenge would be politically tough, with opposition from Britain and the United States, permanent members of the Security Council who could count on many allies, including members of the European Union.

A second option was to find a treaty with a dispute-settlement clause that could allow Mauritius to bring a case to the Court. The obvious treaty was the Convention on the Elimination of Racial Discrimination, or CERD, which might be invoked to argue that the deportation of Liseby Elysé and other Chagossians, and Britain's continuing refusal to allow them to return—set in stone by the MPA—were racially discriminatory acts. This Convention allowed a party to bring proceedings against another at the Court. Indeed, at the time, James Crawford, Paul Reichler and I were working for Georgia on a case it brought to the Court against Russia, under that Convention, alleging racial discrimination against Georgian minorities in the Russian-occupied territories of Abkhazia and South Ossetia. We awaited a decision of the Court on whether it had jurisdiction.

A third possibility was untested: to argue that the British proposal was illegal under the law of the sea convention because it violated Mauritius's fishing rights around Chagos, and because Britain was not the "coastal state" for Chagos, and so had no right to declare a "marine protected area." To succeed, we would have to persuade a court or tribunal that it had jurisdiction to rule on the legality of the detachment of Chagos. Did the law of the sea cover decolonisation and territorial integrity? Could a law of the sea tribunal rule on resolution 1514, or on a question of sovereignty over land? No international court had yet done that.

As Port Louis reflected on the options, WikiLeaks released a vast tranche of US government documents, millions of pages of "Top Secret" papers leaked onto the internet, some of which related to Chagos. Of particular interest was a 2009 cable from the American embassy in London to the State Department in Washington, on the "marine protected area." The document set out the views of Mr.

Colin Roberts, director of overseas territories at the Foreign Office in London. Extolling the virtues of Mr. Miliband's plan for an MPA, modelled on American sanctuaries in Hawaii and the Marianas, Mr. Roberts asserted that it would create "the largest marine reserve in the world," and prohibit all human activity, except on and around the US base at Diego Garcia.

The proposal would create no difficulties for the local population, Mr. Roberts explained, because . . . there were no inhabitants! "We do not regret the removal of the population," the cable reported him telling US counterparts, as it meant there would be "no human footprints" or "Men Fridays" on BIOT's "uninhabited islands." The term "Man Friday" evoked the language of the 1960s, when Britain purposely misled the UN, but this went even further. The marine park offered a further advantage, Mr. Roberts was reported to have informed the Americans: it would "put paid to resettlement claims of the archipelago's former residents."

The document suggested that environmental protection was being harnessed to extinguish forever the Chagossians' ability to return. The environmental lobby was "far more powerful" than the Chagossians' advocates, Mr. Roberts explained, and was supportive. Millionaires' yachts could visit Peros Banhos, but not the Chagossians. Scientists working with the Zoological Society of London and the Chagos Conservation Trust were able to visit the church where Madame Elysé was baptised, but she could not.

This was a document of the kind that stiffens the backbone. It prompted the Chagossians to file a new claim at the High Court in London, Bancoult No. 4. The case challenged the legality of the proposed "MPA" under English law, on the grounds that its purpose was to prevent the return of the Chagossians. This case would be rejected, like many others, on appeal to the Supreme Court in London, but it was not entirely fruitless: the litigation threw up a raft of secret British government documents that Mr. Bancoult and his lawyers made available to Mauritius against the objections of the British government, which asked for them to be returned. No, said Mauritius, the documents were in the public domain, having been referred to in open court. A British minister grumbled that he was "gravely displeased." He was right to be concerned: the documents shone a bright light on Britain's actions and dishonesty between 1963 and 1973, all behind the scenes.

Around this time, the British government revisited the feasibility of life on Chagos. It held a public consultation, in which 98 per cent of participating Chagossians expressed a wish to return. The accountancy firm KPMG examined the options, concluding that a return was feasible—artisanal fishing, small coconut plots and ecotourism could provide jobs—and would have no adverse environmental effects. Yet the British government decided against resettlement, for reasons of "feasibility, defence and security interests and cost." Instead, it announced a package of £40 million to support Chagossians in their lives outside the archipelago, and more "heritage visits."

The Chagossians challenged the decision before the English courts. At the time of writing, Bancoult No. 5 is pending on appeal to the Supreme Court. Four years after the support package was announced, less than half a million pounds had been disbursed. "There is no mechanism currently in place to implement a plan," the British High Commission told Chagossians in Mauritius.

. . .

As London prevaricated, Mauritius explored a twin-track approach to litigation: one case under the law of the sea convention, another on discrimination in The Hague. If these cases produced a positive outcome, other options could follow, including the advisory opinion route, although as things stood, the prospects for that course seemed politically challenging.

Forty-five years after the dismemberment of Mauritius, on a

cold, snowy day in December 2010, Mauritius notified the Foreign Office in London that it had launched arbitration proceedings under the law of the sea convention. The claim asserted that Mr. Miliband's proposed marine park was illegal, a ruse to stop the Chagossians from returning that was dressed up as environmental protection. The application came with a single document annexed: the US diplomatic cable that referenced the "Men Fridays."

As for the case under the discrimination convention, Port Louis decided to wait until The Hague had ruled on whether it had jurisdiction in Georgia's case against Russia. That judgement was handed down on 1 April 2011. The Solicitor-General of Mauritius attended the reading in the Great Hall of Justice, with a briefcase that contained an application to start a discrimination case against Britain.

At an earlier stage the Court had ruled, on a preliminary basis, that it had jurisdiction to order provisional measures in Georgia's case against Russia. That ruling, in 2008, was by a narrow majority supported by eight of the fifteen judges. Two years on, the makeup of the Court had changed, as did the direction it took: a bare majority now ruled in the opposite direction, namely that the Court did not have jurisdiction. This was a legalistic, technical decision: the majority found that Georgia had failed properly to notify Russia of its claim under the discrimination convention. The defect, a matter of form, killed the case, which the Court threw out—sending a signal to Russia that may have influenced its future actions in Ukraine.

The judgement confirmed how crucial the composition of the Court can be, like any judicial body. The law is not something that is applied mechanically, which means that a change of just one or two judges can totally alter the outcome. In February 2010, the British judge—Rosalyn Higgins, who had voted in favour of jurisdiction at the earlier stage—retired, to be succeeded by Christopher Greenwood, generally seen as less open to human rights arguments than his predecessor. Judge Greenwood joined the majority in ruling that Georgia had not persuaded the Court that it had jurisdiction in the case. Two other judges—from Mexico and New Zealand—also took a different view from the one they had taken in the earlier phase. The dissenting judges complained that the approach of the majority was "unrealistic and formalistic."

The decision remains the most disappointing judgement in any case in which I have been involved before the Court. The Mauritian team in The Hague swiftly concluded that the Court as now composed was unlikely to be a fruitful place to litigate against Britain, or to argue that the deportation of the Chagossians was discriminatory and illegal under international law. The solicitor-general of Mauritius returned to Port Louis with the CERD application in his briefcase. It was never filed.

ISTANBUL

This left the law of the sea case. A few weeks after it was filed, Mauritius's ambassador to the UN, Mr. Meeterbhan, and I visited the US State Department's legal adviser and several of his lawyers. The meeting was a courtesy call to explain our case and make clear that Mauritius was not seeking to challenge the US military base at Diego Garcia. Its aim was to establish that Chagos was part of Mauritius, and the Chagossians had the right to return to their homes. The exchanges were friendly, as the American lawyers listened politely and sceptically, then told us that a law of the sea case against Britain would be hopeless.

An arbitration is different from a case before an international court like the International Court of Justice or the Hamburg Tribunal, where the judges have permanent appointments. In arbitration, each tribunal is created to deal with a single case: each party appoints an arbitrator, and the two parties then agree on three other arbitrators. Mauritius nominated the German judge at the

Hamburg Tribunal, Rüdiger Wolfrum, as its party-appointed arbitrator; Britain appointed Christopher Greenwood, its judge at the ICJ. The two countries then agreed on the other arbitrators from South Africa and Tanzania, and a presiding arbitrator, from Australia. It was yet another all-male affair, despite our efforts. The British choice prompted a delay, when it emerged that shortly after being appointed to the Tribunal, Judge Greenwood participated in the Foreign Office's selection process for its new legal adviser. As the new legal adviser was expected to play a role in the arbitration, Prime Minister Ramgoolam—a member of the English Bar—raised concerns about the appointment. "How can Judge Greenwood sit if he played a role in the appointment of a lawyer involved in the case?" he inquired. It was a reasonable question. Professor Greenwood's earlier role in assisting the British government on Iraq, as disclosed in the article in *The Times*, was also a concern, as it was by now known that the war was launched from Diego Garcia. We decided, however, to steer clear of that issue, as it would have required the Tribunal to examine issues it may not want to get into.

Prime Minister Ramgoolam instructed us to challenge Judge Greenwood. This was delicate because James Crawford and I had worked closely with Greenwood; we liked him and had good relations with him. We hoped he might withdraw voluntarily, but he did not do so. The arbitration was suspended as the formal challenge was heard. Each party submitted written statements, supported by expert views, and a day of oral arguments was held at the Peace Palace in The Hague. Sir Sydney Kentridge, who led the Mauritius team, was a distinguished lawyer who had represented Nelson Mandela in the "Treason Trial," five decades earlier, and argued some of Olivier Bancoult's Chagos cases in the English courts. Impartiality turns on a simple test, Kentridge submitted: did the circumstances give rise to "a reasonable apprehension of bias" on the part of a reasonable observer? He cited an opinion submitted by Tom Mensah, the former President of the Hamburg Tribunal, who considered that Greenwood should not sit. Britain disagreed: that test may apply in domestic proceedings, but at the international level the standard was far less stringent, it argued. It relied on opinions from Judges Higgins and Guillaume, two former Presidents of the ICJ, in support of the view that there was no problem with Greenwood sitting.

"Why should this tribunal be content with a lesser standard of impartiality?" Kentridge asked. Judge Greenwood's role in the appointment of the Foreign Office legal adviser indicated a continuing "relationship of trust and confidence" between him and the British government. "We cast no aspersion on Judge Greenwood's integrity," but Kentridge hoped the United Kingdom might reconsider and "allow the Judge to step down with dignity." The UK did not reconsider, and Judge Greenwood did not step down. The four arbitrators came down in favour of Britain's argument, having deliberated for several months, concluding that the "appearance of bias" test did not apply in a law of the sea arbitration. They preferred to apply the standard used by the International Court—although not the one that caused Judge Khan to be unable to sit in the South West Africa cases—and ruled there were no "justifiable grounds" for doubting Judge Greenwood's independence and impartiality: his role in the appointment process was "brief" and did not constitute an "existing relationship" with the British government.

And so the case proceeded, to be hit immediately by another delay: as anticipated, Britain argued that the arbitral tribunal had no jurisdiction, in part because the law of the sea did not allow it to express views on self-determination or resolution 1514, or whether Chagos was a British colony or part of Mauritius. As written pleadings were exchanged, the parties could not agree on where to hold the hearing on jurisdiction. Not in Europe, said Mauritius, the beating heart of colonialism. Not in Buenos Aires or Johannesburg, Britain responded to our suggestions. We settled on Dubai, where

arguments were aired on a scorching day in early 2013. The tribunal took just four days to decide that Britain's objections were so
closely interwoven with the merits of the case that they could not
be decided separately or in advance. The question of jurisdiction
was joined to the merits. This hurdle crossed, the case proceeded to
two rounds of lengthy written pleadings, then a hearing in Istanbul
in a courtroom constructed in the basement of the famous Pera Palace Hotel, favoured by Kemal Atatürk, founder of modern Turkey,
and by crime writer Agatha Christie, who was said to have written
Murder on the Orient Express at the hotel.

The hearing was held in the spring of 2014, arguments and
counter-arguments interrupted by tea breaks, Turkish delight and
walking tours of Istanbul. The two sides occupied different floors
of the hotel, as did the five arbitrators, which made this a hearing
like no other. Matters of maritime law, conservation and colonialism, and the rights of Chagossians, were argued in sight of the
Bosporus.

There were memorable moments.

Conversations shouted across the breakfast room, to avoid any
hint of inappropriate private communication between counsel and
arbitrator.

Early-morning encounters in the gym, with spectacular views
across the Golden Horn, as counsel and arbitrator pedalled furi-
ously on neighbouring machines.

The craftsmanship of the intricate wooden podium constructed
by the hotel's carpenter, with dimensions that fell a little short,
causing papers to perch precariously.

Arguments put with passion. "We have no doubts about our
sovereignty," British Attorney General Dominic Grieve declared,
offering Mauritius discussions on "practical implementation" of the
marine protected area. No law of the sea tribunal could express
views on sovereignty over land, on ownership of Chagos or the
"BIOT," he asserted. As for the coral reefs of Chagos, they were
special and pristine. "As a diver myself," he noted, only a few days

earlier he had been enjoying the waters around the Maldives, a few hundred miles north of Peros Banhos.

There were moments of mirth. On being posed an uncomfortable question by one of the arbitrators, a British lawyer was handed a sheet of paper on which three scrawled words were plainly visible: "DO NOT ANSWER." She ignored the instruction, or maybe did not see it.

There was revelation, as we learned that the main source of pollution around Chagos was the solitary vessel leased to the British government by a company called MRAG, which was given the herculean task of policing a marine protected area spread across half a million square kilometres.

And there was legal argument of a kind and quality that left me feeling happy to be an international lawyer. For many present the standout moment was an exchange between two of the arbitrators and one of Mauritius's counsel on the central issue in the case, the one on which Madame Elysé's future rested: was resolution 1514 and the principle of territorial integrity binding as a matter of international law, and if it was, when precisely did it become binding? Judge Greenwood homed in surgically on the issue: was resolution 1514's requirement to respect territorial integrity already a rule of international law by November 1965, when Chagos was detached, or by March 1968, when Mauritius gained its independence?

Professor Crawford responded. The "territorial integrity rule" was part of the law of self-determination by 1960, he explained: resolution 1514 merely expressed an existing rule, it did not create a new one. The law was reflected in what states did, Crawford added, and what they did included voting for General Assembly resolutions. He offered an analogy. "The appetite comes through eating, if I could quote an Italian maxim." As the arbitrators' faces made clear, it was apparent that no one in the basement of the Pera Palace Hotel understood what he meant, so he clarified: the "territorial integrity" principle was applicable in 1965, when the British acted, and it continued to apply after that, in 1968 and beyond.

In other words, the rule existed when Chagos was detached and when Mauritius gained independence—and it was violated. Moreover, as the documents before the Tribunal made clear, Britain knew full well in 1965 that its conduct was illegal. Instead of giving effect to the rule, Britain took steps to avoid it, and misled the UN by concocting the idea that the islands had no permanent population.

"What about the taking away of the population from the island at that moment?" Judge Wolfrum inquired. The question touched on the situation of Madame Elysé, who was not present with us in the basement of the Pera Palace Hotel. The expulsion of the population was envisaged in 1965 and "an aspect of the illegality," Professor Crawford replied. It was illegal as a part of the project to detach the archipelago and eliminate the population.

The hearings ran for two weeks, the early stages of a modern, truncated Jarndyce and Jarndyce, the case that ran for generations in Dickens's *Bleak House*. Argument, counter-argument, meetings, late-night drafting, walks, drinks, dinners, then a farewell. The hearing closed and attendees returned to homes around the globe.

International Court of Justice, The Hague, 1920s.

. . .

Eleven months passed, then the Permanent Court of Arbitration in The Hague sent word that the ruling would be delivered in March 2015. One step forward, one step sideways. Unanimously, the five arbitrators ruled that the "marine protected area" was established unlawfully, that Britain had violated its obligations to Mauritius under the law of the sea, on fishing, marine resources and seabed minerals. Britain failed to have regard to Mauritius's rights, or to engage in proper consultations with the island nation. The case was not quite as hopeless as the US State Department legal adviser had warned us, but he was not entirely off beam, for the Tribunal declined to rule on which of the two countries was the "coastal state."

Three arbitrators concluded that the law of the sea convention did not allow them to express a view on the territorial sovereignty of the islands of Chagos. Accordingly, they declined to rule which country was the coastal state, or on the effect of resolution 1514, or on the exchanges between Judge Greenwood and Professor Crawford. They passed over in silence on the future of Madame Elysé and other Chagossians, and on the legacy of colonialism. This was the majority view, expressed by arbitrators Shearer, Greenwood and Hoffmann.

Two arbitrators, however, reached a different conclusion. Judges Kateka and Wolfrum concluded that the Tribunal could decide which country was the coastal state for Chagos, and in their view it was Mauritius, not the United Kingdom. The two arbitrators expressed their dissent on the merits, opening the way—maybe as Judge Jessup did in the South West Africa cases five decades earlier—to the intelligence of a future day.

This is what they concluded:

In 1965 Chagos was part of the territory of the colony of Mauritius.

Resolution 1514 reflected international law when Chagos was detached, and it included a binding obligation to maintain territorial integrity.

Mauritius did not consent to the detachment.

Harold Wilson resorted to the language of intimidation—"frighten them with hope"—and threatened Premier Ramgoolam, who was subject to "duress."

The detachment of Chagos, a part of the colony of Mauritius, violated international law and was without legal effect. It violated the law of decolonisation, reflected in resolution 1514, and the right of self-determination.

Moreover, there were "disturbing similarities" between the establishment of BIOT in 1965 and the proclamation of the MPA in 2010. In both instances, Britain had disregarded the rights of Mauritius: "the United Kingdom did violate the standard of good faith."

· · ·

The result was both positive and disappointing. Positive, because the Tribunal had ruled the proposed MPA to be illegal; disappointing, because the majority said nothing about sovereignty. Nevertheless, as I have come to learn, in the law, as in life, nothing is ever only what it seems: the real-world consequences of a ruling, including the rippling effects of a decent dissent, can take time to work their magic. For the first time, two international judges had spoken in favour of the claim put by Mauritius, and none had opposed that claim. The majority maintained a discreet silence on the merits of the British claim.

In this way, Judges Kateka and Wolfrum opened another door, just as the dissenting judges had done in 1966, in respect of Namibia. I have learned not to react instantly to a judgement, to allow the dust to fall and to settle, to await the future possibilities. So it might yet be for Chagos.

NEW YORK

After the Tribunal declared the Chagos marine protected area to have been illegally established, I returned to Port Louis to discuss the award's implications for the other unresolved issue. A new government was now in office, led by Sir Anerood Jugnauth, who had attended the Lancaster House conference back in 1965 and was now serving his third term as Prime Minister.

"What are the legal options?" he inquired. A man of deliberate authority, and much decorated by the British, Sir Anerood was passionate about Chagos and the rights of its former inhabitants. The struggle continues, he stated, impressed by the clarity of the joint dissent of Judges Kateka and Wolfrum. "Is there a route to The Hague?"

The decision of the Court, some years back, to decline jurisdiction in the Georgia case against Russia had left us feeling sceptical about The Hague. However, the Court had recently given judgement in another case in which James Crawford and I were involved, one that softened the edges of our anxieties. The case was brought by Australia, to challenge Japan's scientific whaling programme in the Antarctic. For years commercial whaling had been banned by an international treaty, but an exception allowed whaling for "purposes of scientific research." Japan had relied on this for many years, and now wished to run a programme to catch several hundred fin, humpback and minke whales in the Antarctic. Australia considered Japan's "Whale Research Program" to be a fig leaf, one that was not really about scientific research. It brought a case to The Hague.

At the heart of the case were two questions: What is science? Is Japan's programme "scientific research"? The questions required the Court to take a deep dive into matters of science and fact, something it had previously avoided. In 1997, in the *Gabčíkovo-Nagymaros* case, between Hungary and Slovakia, the Court had bypassed the parties' arguments on the environmental effects of two barrages on the Danube, on water quality and biodiversity. In 2010, in the *Pulp Mills* case, Argentina had sued Uruguay for damaging the River Uruguay allegedly caused by two paper mills. Again, the Court bypassed the issues of hard science, taking refuge in findings of fact by the World Bank's International Finance Corporation.

As counsel in both cases, I had seen how the judges bypassed complex technical arguments. That left me somewhat sceptical about the willingness of the judges to roll up their sleeves and get their hands dirty on Japanese whaling. I was wrong. I observed intense questioning by well-prepared judges, and a fine cross-examination by the Solicitor-General of Australia, who cast aside diplomatic niceties and shredded the expert evidence tendered by Japan's main scientific witness, a delightful Norwegian medical doctor who did not seem to appreciate the extent of the disaster that had befallen his argument. The effect in the Great Hall was extraordinary: in less than thirty minutes, those present observed the collapse of Japan's case on science, allowing the Court to pick up the pieces and rule decisively against Japan, thus settling a complex evidentiary dispute.

The judgement suggested that the Court had entered a new phase. Perhaps this Court might actually be willing to address Chagos, with its historical and factual issues, and sensitive political interests. If we could find a way to get Chagos before the Court, which still seemed hard to imagine, the judges might form a view about the events of the 1960s, not least whether the leaders of soon-to-be-independent Mauritius genuinely consented to the dismemberment of their land. Perhaps the dissent of Kateka and Wolfrum could become a majority view, just as Jessup's dissent in 1966 became the majority view just five years later.

. . .

Prime Minister Jugnauth left us with no wiggle room: "I instruct you to find a route to The Hague," he told us. There was only one route, considered and rejected five years earlier, as the political hurdles then appeared insurmountable: to persuade the General Assembly to request an advisory opinion from the Court on Chagos. We laid out the difficulties.

We would need to formulate legal questions that fell within the competence of the General Assembly.

We would have to put Chagos on the agenda of the General Assembly, something that had not occurred since 1968.

We would need to persuade a majority of UN members that Chagos was not a bilateral territorial dispute between Britain and Mauritius, on which the General Assembly had no authority, but rather a matter of multilateral concern about decolonisation, on which the Assembly did have a role.

We would have to persuade a majority of UN members to vote to send our questions to The Hague, in the face of British and American objections.

If each of these obstacles could be overcome, we would then have to persuade a majority of the judges that the Court had jurisdiction, should exercise it and give an opinion.

Finally, we would need to persuade a majority of judges that resolution 1514, with its commitment to self-determination and territorial integrity, reflected a rule of international law in November 1965; that Chagos was part of the colony of Mauritius; and that its detachment was contrary to international law because Mauritius had not given consent.

"A tall order," one minister remarked, with a grin.

"Indeed," Prime Minister Jugnauth responded. "But the situation is changed: now we have some support, the view of two respected international judges, that the excision of Chagos and the dismemberment of Mauritius were unlawful." The dissenting opinion of Judges Kateka and Wolfrum was central to his thinking.

The Prime Minister instructed us to prepare questions to go to the Court. He appointed an experienced career diplomat to return to the UN: Jagdish Koonjul was there in 2002, when Mauritius was on the Security Council in the run-up to the Iraq war. Highly regarded, and well placed to navigate a path through arcane and complicated UN rules and procedures, he was smart, energetic, long-haired and wore many rings on the fingers of both hands.

. . .

We spent part of the spring of 2016 attending to the Prime Minister's instructions. In Washington, DC, James Crawford, Paul Reichler and I met in a coffee shop near the White House to talk through possible draft questions for the Court. The first draft—written on a series of Starbucks napkins—sought to imagine questions that were not too general or political, or which might allow the Court to avoid giving meaningful answers, as it had done in recent advisory opinions on nuclear weapons and the independence of Kosovo. The key to a decent question, we knew, was that it must be simple, narrowly focused, without ambiguity, and capable of being answered with a straight yes or no.

Ambassador Koonjul identified options to put Chagos on the agenda of the General Assembly. The path of least resistance, he concluded, was via the "General Committee," a body made up of twenty-six delegates who broadly represented the UN's full membership. Able to put an item on the Assembly's agenda, for discussion and vote, the General Committee generally operated by consensus.

In September 2016, Ambassador Koonjul managed to put Chagos onto the General Committee's agenda—for the first time in fifty years. He was assisted by a dramatic intervening event that occurred a few weeks earlier—Britain voted in a referendum to leave the European Union. This had unexpected and immediate consequences: as British government ministers waxed lyrical about a new "Empire 2.0" and alliances with Commonwealth countries, the brutal reality was that London suddenly discovered it could no longer rely on the unqualified support of EU members and their networks across the UN. Beyond the EU too, Britain's authority suffered a major collapse.

As the General Committee meeting approached, Ambassador Koonjul sensed that Mauritius might be able to obtain the support of thirteen of the twenty-six members, just short of a majority. Britain was not sure it could rely on the support of all other members, as some might abstain or be absent. Three possibilities opened up: Mauritius could push for a vote, which would be unusual for a Committee that acted by consensus; it could put the matter off for a month, in the hope that a majority could be garnered; or it could accept the offer from the President of the General Assembly, proposed by Britain, to defer the matter for a year in return for a commitment that Chagos would feature on the General Assembly's agenda after May 2017.

Each option had risks.

An immediate vote could be lost, and it would then be difficult to get Chagos back on the Committee's agenda.

A month's delay might allow Britain time to lobby and win more support.

Delay for a year, with agreement that the Assembly would then vote on a request for an advisory opinion, would give the British even more time to lobby.

The options required reflection, and we talked the issues through for hours, pushing and pulling in different directions. Paul Reichler and I eventually settled on what we considered to be the least dangerous option: delay for a year. Ambassador Koonjul agreed, hopeful that support from African countries and others in the Non-Aligned Movement would be consolidated. Yet, he counselled, nothing was certain, and the final vote would be difficult.

Prime Minister Jugnauth was not thrilled with our advice, preferring an immediate vote. "Let us take our chance now." Ambassador Koonjul arranged urgent phone conversations, which Paul and I participated in from the bowels of the Washington Nationals baseball stadium, amid much chanting and roaring. The Prime Minister pushed back. "Time is not on my side." He chuckled. "I'm eighty-six, I've waited fifty years for this moment!" Eventually, he accepted our advice, disappointed. "Nine more months? I suppose that's bearable."

Mauritius and Britain agreed to defer the matter until the following summer, assisted by the Assembly's President, a Fijian diplomat, who expressed the hope that time might allow the two countries to resolve their differences. Chagos would feature on the agenda of the 71st General Assembly, as Item 87 ("Request for an advisory opinion of the International Court of Justice on the legal consequences of the separation of the Chagos Archipelago from Mauritius in 1965"), with no action to be taken before 1 June 2017. Mauritius made clear that if there was no progress by the end of May it would present a draft resolution and seek a vote.

Talks followed, without progress. A meeting took place in the margins of the General Assembly's annual meeting, when the Mauritian Prime Minister was assured by Britain's new Foreign Secretary, on the basis of nothing much, that all would be well. Boris Johnson failed to mention that Britain was about to announce a support package of £40 million, to improve the lives of Chagossians. To learn this from the press, a few days later, did not enhance the sense that Mr. Johnson was a reliable interlocutor.

Mr. Johnson failed to mention other matters. He passed in silence on the pressure Britain was about to place on Chagossians living in Britain to return to Mauritius or the Seychelles, part of a broader attack on unwelcome immigrants. Nor did he mention the extension of the US lease at Diego Garcia for a further twenty years, after its initial term expired in December 2016. That very month, I observed first-hand Mr. Johnson's skittishness on the matter of Chagos at a diplomatic reception at Buckingham Palace. I had known Johnson, who was Foreign Secretary at the time, for many years, but my effort to introduce him to Mauritius's High Commissioner in London fell flat, as the Foreign Secretary looked down at his shoes ("always a sign of shiftiness," a friend remarked) and offered an uncomfortable shake of the hand, then did "a runner."

In February 2017, senior officials from Britain and Mauritius met in London, without progress.

In March the British government announced more "heritage visits" for Chagossians. Madame Elysé did not wish to go, Olivier Bancoult told me, nor did any of his clients.

In April, Paul, Jagdish and I met with Sean Murphy, a new member of the team, in Washington, DC (James Crawford having been elected a judge at the Court, he resigned from our team). We spent several hours tinkering with the drafts of two questions for the Assembly to send to the Court.

In May, in the shadow of a general election, the British government made clear it would vigorously oppose the questions being sent to The Hague. An advisory opinion would be an "abuse" of the Court. They were supported by the Americans, who considered the exercise to be "excessive."

The African Union, on the other hand, resolved to commit its members to support an advisory opinion on Chagos. So did the Non-Aligned Movement.

The battle lines drawn, Britain proposed to send a high-level delegation to Port Louis, hoping to extend the failed talks into June. Mauritius declined, ever polite but increasingly firm.

At the end of May, time ran out.

RESOLUTION 71/292

On 1 June 2017, Mauritius requested that the General Assembly take action on Chagos. A debate was scheduled at the Assembly for the end of the month, to be followed by a vote. Mauritius circulated an informal draft resolution, a request for an advisory opinion with the two questions we had drafted. Was the decolonisation of Mauritius lawfully completed? If not, what were the legal consequences? A "position paper" set out the history and the arguments in favour of a resolution.

Reports came in that Britain was engaged in "heavy campaigning" in New York, and lobbying capitals around the world to vote against the resolution. Latin American countries that had lost cases at the Court, like Colombia, were said to be favoured targets. In a letter to all the UN members, Britain set out its stall: Chagos was a bilateral dispute between the two countries, for them to resolve—it was not a multilateral matter on decolonisation, so the General Assembly had no authority to request an opinion from the Court.

The attitudes of Russia and China would be significant. Both had territorial issues of their own to worry about—Crimea and the South China Seas, respectively—and would take comfort that an advisory opinion on Chagos would set no precedent. Our aim was to ring-fence Chagos, to treat it as a discrete issue of decolonisation, not about territorial sovereignty, and to make clear that a dispute which was purely about territorial sovereignty could not be the subject of an advisory opinion request. On this basis, both countries indicated they would not oppose the resolution, helpfully for our side. Russia suggested (and obtained) a modest change to one of the draft questions, to make even clearer the distinction between Chagos—a decolonisation issue—and other territorial situations that were not connected to colonialism.

Another key issue to be neutralised was the future of the US base at Diego Garcia, the old "Camp Justice" where Bob Hope once performed. This was important for many countries and also, if we got to The Hague, for the judges, who would not want to be accused of being asked to close a major American military base. Mauritius circulated a note to all UN members, confirming once more that it supported the continued operation of the base at Diego Garcia in accordance with international law. Later, Mauritius went a step further, offering the United States a ninety-nine-year lease.

Fake news abounded, as word arrived that British diplomats were stoking up rumours that Mauritius wanted to lease the base—or another Chagos island—to China. The claim was nonsense and easily swatted away.

There followed days of intense argument and counter-argument. If Britain put out a position paper, Mauritius rebutted it, and vice versa. We sensed a growing British anxiety, reflected in the continued spread of rumours and suggestions that had no basis in fact. As the date for the vote approached, Boris Johnson telephoned Mr. Jugnauth and asked him to abandon the initiative. Characteristically ill-prepared, the British Foreign Secretary went off script and threatened economic and other consequences if the vote proceeded. Are you breaking the long-established understanding that Chagos is ring-fenced as an issue between the two countries, the Prime Minister of Mauritius inquired? Mr. Johnson quickly changed tack.

A week before the vote, the Congo (Brazzaville) circulated a draft resolution with our two questions, on behalf of the UN's Group of African States. It included the modest Russian amendment. The following day, the Non-Aligned Movement—a creature

View of Diego Garcia from US Air Force plane, 1970s.

of decolonisation, established in Bandung in Indonesia six decades earlier—urged support for the resolution. Two of its members, Chile and Colombia, who were thought to be leaning towards the British position, did not oppose.

Nikki Haley, the US ambassador to the UN, chose the moment to reach out to the full UN membership. It was "inappropriate" to seek an advisory opinion on a bilateral dispute when one party to the dispute did not consent. The vote would set "a dangerous precedent."

Four days before the vote, Anerood Jugnauth arrived in New York, leading a delegation from Mauritius, accompanied by a group of Chagossians. Liseby Elysé was not there, although her nephew Olivier Bancoult was, with her friend Janine Sadrien. They attended the opening of a small exhibition of photographs about the Chagossian experience, in the lobby of the UN headquarters. "The holding of the exhibit in UN premises does not imply endorsement by the United Nations," a notice proclaimed.

Three days before the vote, we received word that Britain and the United States were intensifying the pressure at senior government levels. A British minister arrived in New York armed with a "non paper," the familiar arguments set out in bold. "This is a precedent we should avoid setting." The message coincided with a shift in the British tack, as it moved to encourage abstentions to limit the size of the vote in favour of the resolution. The British ambassador reportedly invited forty Asian and Pacific countries to a meeting on Chagos, but fewer than a dozen turned up, and only four ambassadors.

The day before the vote, I was in New York for last-minute lobbying with the Mauritian team. The Non-Aligned Movement had by now called on all its members to support the resolution. Britain warned that the General Assembly was being used, "a back door route to the Court," which risked "compromising" the judicial institution.

I spent a long and fascinating day at the UN headquarters,

many hours seated at a small table in the Indonesia Lounge, meeting delegates to talk about the resolution. I met with dozens of individuals, mostly legal advisers, some my former students. Across the day, only two delegates—a genial Australian and a sensitive Canadian—expressed any inclination to support Britain, albeit with little enthusiasm. Most of the delegates were from Africa, Asia and the Caribbean; none were hostile to Britain, all indicated they had come under pressure, and none suggested they might succumb. Many mentioned Britain's inability to let go of its colonial instinct.

My brief was to offer reassurance. Support for the resolution, or abstention, would not set a precedent, as other situations were not about decolonisation. Support for the resolution would not damage the UN or the Court. The vote was simply about the integrity of resolution 1514, and the General Assembly's authority. Chagos was a decolonisation matter, different from Crimea or the South China Seas, and the Falklands/Malvinas. Chagos was about the territorial integrity of former colonies, and the rights of their inhabitants.

I learned a great deal that day, not least about the decline in Britain's authority at the world body. I observed more than a few minutely raised eyebrows, if the British Foreign Secretary's name came up. His propensity to use racist epithets was widely known— a number of African delegates referenced articles he had written in the *Daily Telegraph*, and others mentioned his racially charged put-down of President Obama, in the *Sun* newspaper ("the part-Kenyan president's ancestral dislike of the British Empire"). In this multilateral forum, in an age in which media articles have a global reach, Mr. Johnson and his writings offered useful support for Mauritius.

I flew back to London late in the evening, for a family commitment. On the flight, it seemed possible—yet still barely imaginable—that the Court would shortly get a chance to rule on Chagos. If a life in the courtrooms of the world teaches you anything, it is that nothing is ever to be taken for granted.

PART FIVE

·——◆——·

2019

"While the first liberation struggle might be against the coloniser, the second, inevitably, is against ourselves."

—SARA COLLINS, on the occasion of the PEN Pinter Prize being awarded to Tsitsi Dangarembga, British Library, September 2021

On the morning of 22 June 2017, Sir Anerood Jugnauth made his way to the podium to address the General Assembly. Eighty-seven years old, dark-haired, intent, the humble grandson of economic migrants from India, the former Prime Minister of Mauritius had waited a long time for this moment.

He had started life as a government clerk in Port Louis, working for the Poor Law Department of the British colony of Mauritius. A scholarship sent him to London, to become a barrister of Lincoln's Inn, and on his return to Port Louis he was elected to the Legislative Council. In September 1965, he returned

to London as a member of the Mauritius delegation at the Lancaster House conference. In due course he became a political leader, then Prime Minister, once, twice and for a third term. In September 1982, he first stood at the General Assembly's podium to issue a public call for Chagos to be recognised as part of Mauritius, and for the Chagossians to be allowed to return. Thirty-five years on, with his son Pravind now Prime Minister, this would be his final address to the Assembly.

He spoke soberly, with understatement, paying tribute to Madame Elysé and the Chagossians who had travelled with him

to New York. The only living survivor of the Lancaster House conference, he knew all about duress and Britain's "blatant violation
of international law," a personal matter. He urged a vote for the
resolution, to complete decolonisation, to respect the international
rule of law.

Twenty-three countries spoke in the debate, most in support
of the resolution. Britain's ambassador, Matthew Rycroft, was one
of the few to oppose. I knew the name, as back in January 2003,
when he served as Tony Blair's private secretary, he had expressed
irritation with a note by Attorney General Lord Goldsmith rec-
ommending a further Security Council resolution to authorise
the use of force in Iraq. "Specifically said we did not need further
advice this week," Mr. Rycroft scribbled. His commitment to international law did not seem to have firmed up in the intervening
years. Resettlement on Chagos was impossible, he told the General
Assembly, suggesting (without any evidence) that Mauritius was
using the Chagossians to buttress a claim to sovereignty. The US
representative, who spoke later, offered a rare note of support.

The debate ran across the full morning. In London the legal
team watched online as the vote followed, as did Madame Elysé in
Port Louis. Green in favour of the resolution; red against; yellow an
abstention; black for absence from the chamber. In an instant the
board flashed generally green, an indication that resolution 71/292
had passed with a large majority. Ninety-four countries voted in
favour, just sixteen voted against, including Australia and New Zealand, two of the four former British colonies that supported Britain.
Sixty-five countries abstained, including China, Russia and France,
and nineteen countries were absent. Of the twenty-seven EU members, Cyprus supported the resolution, Croatia and Hungary voted
against, the rest abstained. Three of the fifty-four Commonwealth
members supported Britain. Brazil, India and South Africa led support for the resolution, and only two developing countries voted
against: Afghanistan and the Maldives. No country from Africa,

Latin America or the Caribbean supported Britain. It was not so much Global Britain, perhaps, as Little Britain.

The General Assembly voted to send two questions to The Hague, the twenty-fifth advisory opinion requested of the Court. The first question asked the Court to determine whether, in 1968, the decolonisation of Mauritius was completed in accordance with international law, given the separation of Chagos. If the answer was "no," the second question addressed the consequences of Britain's continued administration of Chagos, and the resettlement of the Chagossians. Chagos, resolution 1514 and territorial integrity would be argued before the Court.

In New York, Madame Elysé's friend Janine was thrilled. "I cried out. I was so happy, so emotional, I shrieked! My country, my Chagos, we are not alone, we felt surrounded by supporters."

In Mauritius the Chagossians' colleagues were elated. "I could not imagine such happiness," Madame Elysé would say, "that the world had heard us, that we were not alone."

THE ELECTION

The UN secretariat transmitted the two questions to The Hague. The Court issued a press release. The case now had a name—the "Legal Consequences of the Separation of the Chagos Archipelago from Mauritius in 1965"—and a timetable: the UN and any member could file a written statement with the Court by the end of January 2018, followed by written responses to the arguments of others, to be filed in April. Madame Elysé's hopes rested with the Court's fifteen judges.

The South West Africa judgements of 1966 confirmed the significance of the Court's composition, how an outcome could turn on the presence or absence of one or two judges, and the proclivities of individual judges and the working of the group as a whole. In preparing a case, as I learned from James Crawford, you must consider

with care the background and propensities of each judge: their previous rulings and extra-judicial writings, their country's views on
matters that may touch on the case. One or two judges can change
the direction of travel, as the Georgia case had shown, and Chagos
was no exception. By the time the case reached The Hague, Crawford, who had long advised Mauritius, had been elected a judge at
the Court, which meant that only fourteen judges would sit (and
the first permanent Australian judge since Percy Spender would
be excluded). We assumed Judge Greenwood would not sit, as he
had served as an arbitrator in the earlier MPA case, but received
no word from the Court on that. In the meantime, however, Iraq,
Brexit and Chagos would combine to effect a significant change in
the Court's composition.

Shortly after the adoption of resolution 71/292, Judge Greenwood was up for reelection to the Court. Since 1945, Britain had
always had a judge on the Court: seven candidates for election,
every one of them successful. It was hard to imagine Britain not
having a judge. This I was taught back in 1982, and forty years on
the idea seemed set in stone.

In November 2017, elections to the International Court of Justice were held at the UN, with six candidates for five slots, only one
of whom was not a sitting judge; the judges from Somalia, France
and Brazil were promptly reelected, and an outside candidate, from
Lebanon, took the fourth slot. That left two candidates competing
for a single position: Judge Greenwood from Britain, and Judge
Bhandari from India.

The UN elects the ICJ judges with a system that requires a double majority, of votes cast by the General Assembly and the Security
Council. In the first round of voting, the Indian candidate was
ahead in the Assembly, but the Council inclined strongly towards
the British candidate. The stalemate led to further rounds of voting,
to continue until one candidate was ahead in both bodies.

For Mauritius, the choice presented a delicate situation. In their generally good relations with India and Britain, the Chagos issue had introduced a note of tension with the latter, whereas India was keenly supportive on completing decolonisation. It was reasonable to assume that an Indian judge would view the arguments of Mauritius more favourably, and whereas Judge Greenwood was highly regarded as a judge, he was considered to have a conservative disposition on matters of human rights. "To listen to Chris Greenwood is like drinking endless streams of hot chocolate," my late friend Jonathan Cooper once told a group of Foreign Office diplomats. For the government of Mauritius, the situation was clear: presented with a choice, it would opt for Judge Bhandari.

As voting between the two candidates proceeded in the General Assembly, the first round had the Indian ahead of his British counterpart by 110 votes to 79. As the voting continued, the United States intervened with an email sent to most UN members, but apparently not India, affirming its "strong support" for Judge Greenwood, noting that he had recused himself from the Chagos advisory opinion. The information, which was news to Mauritius, had the unintended consequence of putting the Chagos issue squarely into the debate. The US communication, therefore, did not increase support for the British candidate, so that by the fifth round of voting the Indian candidate's lead had increased, the vote now standing at 121 to 68. In the Security Council, on the other hand, Judge Greenwood was consistently ahead, by nine votes to five, with one abstention. At that point, it was decided to pause the election, to allow further consultations with capitals.

Britain's permanent representative had circulated a letter to the membership, extolling the British candidate's "outstanding service" to the Court. This too mentioned Chagos, and the decision on recusal, which further reinforced the issue. As India and Britain lobbied, London proposed the use of a joint conference between the Security Council and General Assembly, a rare procedure to break the deadlock.

The idea collapsed when the Americans suddenly changed course, withdrawing a letter circulated in support of the British candidate. Apparently this was at the insistence of US Ambassador Nikki Haley, following an intervention by India after it learned of the letter's existence, unhappy with its conflict on America's stated position of neutrality between the two candidates. President Donald Trump's friendship with the Indian premier, Narendra Modi, left Britain's "special relationship" with the United States a little less "special." The withdrawal of the US letter sent a signal, in effect sealing the result. The British candidacy was withdrawn.

The loss of the British judge was widely reported; it was seen as a disaster in London, as the government sought to pass the buck and blame civil servants for a "failure of UK diplomacy." The reality was different, as many observers knew: Britain had lost its judge on the International Tribunal for the Law of the Sea (ITLOS) many years earlier, after the Iraq war, and they had now lost their ICJ judge because of the toxic combination of Iraq, Brexit, Chagos and Mr. Johnson. Five decades after the 1966 South West Africa judgements, Britain's bubble was burst, reflected in the loss of two big votes at the General Assembly. If losing one vote at the UN may be written off as carelessness, to lose two in quick succession reflects something even more serious.

THE PLEADINGS

And so the composition of the Court changed. There was a new Lebanese judge, the Indian judge was reelected and, for the first time in its history, no British judge would sit on the Court. This was the background against which the Mauritius team started to draft its written submissions. To present a case is to tell a story, and to do so in such a way that it can connect to judges from many different countries.

The story is presented in different forms, initially written, and then, in the hearing, by way of spoken words. Images also play a role. As the proceedings unfold, with different parties reacting to the story, the presentations evolve, becoming more narrowly focused on particular issues. The law offers a framework within which the story is set out, but I have come to understand that how the facts are presented can influence the reaction of an individual judge. A case has many audiences—governments, the public, the media—but in writing a pleading, the only audience that really matters is the judges.

In an advisory opinion, the first document is called "The Written Statement," a chance to set out your case. Mauritius had aired its arguments in the earlier law of the sea arbitration on the MPA, but the judges in The Hague were different, and they would expect the material to be laid out in response to the two questions sent from New York. "Keep it simple," James Crawford had told me, before my first case at the Court a quarter of a century earlier—make sure the narrative is clear and accessible for each judge, conscious of their cultures and beliefs, not just in law, and ensure it comes with a road map. Lay out a series of propositions, then hammer them home:

The Court has jurisdiction.

There is no reason it cannot be exercised.

Self-determination is articulated in resolution 1514, which reflected the law already in 1965, when Chagos was detached.

The law included a principle of territorial integrity, to prohibit the detachment of any part of a colony without the consent of the colonised.

In 1965, Chagos was part of the territory of the British colony of Mauritius.

The people of Mauritius had no opportunity to express consent to detachment.

The detachment and removal of the inhabitants was achieved by duplicitous means.

The detachment was unlawful and had no legal effects.
Decolonisation was not completed.
Madame Elysé and the Chagossians were wrongly removed from
    their homes.

Each proposition required evidence on the facts, and submissions on the law, like any case. This one, however, had a distinct and powerful human element, one that was required to be presented to the Court. How could the Chagossians tell their story to the Court? Advisory opinion proceedings generally do not have witnesses, so we reflected on how the voices of the Chagossians might be heard in the Great Hall of Justice.

There were other considerations to think through. Britain would argue that Chagos was a bilateral dispute between two countries and not properly the subject of an advisory opinion, so it would be helpful to have many countries participate to reflect a global interest. Port Louis moved to encourage such participation, reaching out to presidents and prime ministers, holding meetings in New York and visiting capitals. We convened a meeting of two dozen countries in The Hague, to explain the case and its broader political or legal significance.

The outreach seemed to work. Thirty-one countries filed Written Statements, along with the African Union, which spoke with a single voice on behalf of the entire continent of fifty-five countries. Countries from all five UN regional groups participated, reflecting a population of over a billion human beings. Such numbers tend not to care about bilateral sovereignty disputes. Eight countries from Africa participated; six from the Asia-Pacific region; eight from the "western Europe and others group," including two eastern European countries; and seven from Latin America and the Caribbean.

The first round of Written Statements overwhelmingly supported the positions taken by Mauritius.

Only one country argued that the Court had no jurisdiction: Australia.

Five countries accepted the Court had jurisdiction, but urged that it should decline to exercise it: Britain and the United States, along with Chile, France and Israel. To exercise jurisdiction and answer the two questions, they argued, would trespass into the forbidden domain of a bilateral dispute.

China, Russia and Germany disagreed. Chagos *was* about decolonisation and properly a matter for the General Assembly, so the Court should answer both questions, albeit with restraint.

On the merits, Britain and the United States stood alone. No country supported their arguments that self-determination was not already a right under international law at the time when Chagos was detached, and when Mauritius became independent.

Every other Written Statement that addressed the matter concluded that self-determination was part of international law when Britain detached Chagos, and that Britain had violated the principle of territorial integrity. The decolonisation of Mauritius remained incomplete: Chagos was part of Mauritius, not Britain.

Not one Written Statement—not from Britain or the US, or even Australia—challenged the proposition that if the decolonisation of Mauritius was not complete, it must be completed immediately. Nor did these countries oppose the proposition that the completion of decolonisation meant that Madame Elysé would be entitled to return to Peros Banhos.

In May 2019, ten countries and the African Union filed a second round of arguments, Written Comments to respond to the first round of arguments. These documents were shorter, more narrowly focused, addressing specific points of disagreement, Britain and the United States on one side, Mauritius and seven others, and the entire continent of Africa, on the other.

In the second round, Mauritius included the personal experiences of five Chagossians, written accounts of forcible removals and a desire to return. One such account was submitted by Madame Elysé. The other accounts came from Marie Mimose Furcy, also from Peros Banhos, and Rosemonde Berthin, Marie Janine Sadrien and Louis Rosemond Samynaden, from Salomon island. Britain could have included the views of Chagossians living in the United Kingdom, but chose not to, so these were the only Chagossian views presented directly to the Court.

With the close of the written phase, the procedure moved to the hearing, where arguments would be aired in open court. A hearing is a moment of theatre, and we wanted the Court to hear many different voices in support of Mauritius, and fewer voices in opposition. This too required active preparation.

MADAME ELYSÉ, 2018

Twenty-two countries and the African Union expressed a desire to participate in the hearings. The Court allowed each participant forty-five minutes to speak, although Mauritius and Britain were each allocated an extra two hours, given their particular interest in the case. This was a full three-hour session, minus twenty minutes for the customary coffee break.

How would we use our time? There was fact and law and a story to tell, the events before the separation of Chagos and those that followed. Our main task was to persuade the Court that resolution 1514, with its references to self-determination and territorial integrity, represented the law in 1965, and that it was violated. The subject was dry, to be sure, but it did not have to be presented in a dull way. There was a human story to be told, and early on we concluded that the judges must hear a voice from Chagos.

One of our colleagues, Remi Reichhold, travelled from London to Port Louis to meet with each of the five Chagossians who had prepared personal statements, to identify the one who might address the Court most persuasively. His conversations narrowed the options to a choice between Rosemond Samynaden and Liseby Elysé. Normally, one or both would speak from a prepared text, but as neither could read, this presented a challenge: to ad-lib might be risky, as the speaker could head off in an unexpected direction or speak for too long. So we opted for a different approach, to film the statement in advance and seek the Court's permission to play the video in court. The Court granted permission.

"They asked me if I could make a statement before the Court," Madame Elysé explained. "I wanted to contribute." As the case moved through its various stages, she felt a growing sense of optimism, but she wanted to keep those feelings in check. "Two thousand eighteen was a big year for me. I was sixty-five years old, and had stopped working, after twenty-seven years in service as a maid for a Mauritius-Chinese family. I felt as strongly as ever about what had happened to me, I wanted to do what I could to help the case."

In Port Louis, Remi prepared the videos, spending hours with Monsieur Rosemond Samynaden and Madame Elysé. "They were both nervous, but Liseby Elysé the more so." Each took their turn in a large meeting room, seated before a camera, a green screen behind. Rosemond went first, speaking for ten minutes on being expelled and still hoping to return. "I want to die peacefully in Chagos one day."

Madame Elysé had thought carefully about what she would say and talked about it with friends and family. "A video was easier for me. I cannot read." Remi appreciated the time they spent together. "She was visibly anxious, her arms were shaking. I gave very little direction, just asked her to look at the camera and recount her experience. Although I could not understand every word, because she spoke in Creole, her voice was full of emotion. As she told her story, the emotion intensified—pain and anger—and she started to cry. We stopped filming and comforted her. I told her she did not have to do this, but she wanted to go again. The second time, exactly the same thing happened. And again the third. This time, we did not stop filming and let her finish her statement, her right hand covering her face, as tears streamed down her face."

LA COUR!

The hearings were held in September 2018, on four warm, late-summer days, morning and afternoon sessions. We hoped for support from each continent, and for a European Union member to speak on our behalf, and none to speak against; we hoped that China, France and Russia would be absent, that the African Union would speak; and we hoped that Brazil, India and South Africa, the rising powers, would address the Court and speak in our favour.

Our aspirations were driven in part by the composition of the Court, with fourteen judges sitting: five from Europe and North America, four from Asia, three from Africa, and two from Latin America and the Caribbean. The optics were important, hoping to encourage judges to set aside any jurisdictional hurdles, to roll up their sleeves and get their hands dirty on the muck of colonialism and its legacies. We wanted the British and Americans to look isolated, to be seen to be arguing against the grain of history. We wanted the Court to recall the disaster of South West Africa.

It was not just the attendance of countries that was important, but who turned up to argue for them. Advocates before the Court tend to be drawn from a small and unrepresentative group—mostly they are from the North, white, male; a French friend who appears often before the Court happily describes his *confrères* as a "mafia." For this case, we wanted the advocates to be drawn from a more globally representative group. It was like creating a new orchestra, with Ambassador Koonjul our conductor, directing from New York, a lobbying effort that encouraged us to draw on personal contacts in identifying potential counsel. Once more we organised meetings, at the UN and in capitals. We wrote letters and made phone calls. We gathered allies in The Hague, addressed by Prime Minister Pravind Jugnauth.

As the hearing approached, we ticked off the various boxes. Every continent would be there to argue in support of our position. The Attorney General of Cyprus would be present, with advocates for the African Union, Brazil, India and South Africa. China, France and Russia decided not to participate, a way of signalling they did not oppose the case. Lawyers from around the globe arrived in The Hague, many acting *pro bono*. A Japanese academic colleague—the most impressive of Japan's advocates in the case of his country's scientific whaling programme in the Antarctic—made the long journey from Kyoto to argue for Botswana, in French.

. . .

The Mauritius team arrived in The Hague a few days before the hearings, the largest of the twenty-three delegations. Madame Elysé was there, identified in Court papers as a "representative of the Chagossian community." "I really wanted to come, to explain my journey to the judges, to show what my story means at the human level. I came to The Hague to get my island back. I wasn't scared. I had no fear. I had no anxiety."

She had crossed a Rubicon many years earlier, when she started to be involved in the Chagos Group, during the "heritage visit" to Peros Banhos and its cemetery. "That visit was what made me more active, as I became involved in Olivier's cases." Her nephew, Monsieur Bancoult, joined us in The Hague, one of several Chagossians who made the long journey from Port Louis, a resolute and purposeful man who had litigated, over two long decades, five cases for the Chagos Refugee Group before the English courts, up to the Supreme Court and beyond, to Strasbourg, largely without success. A large and distinguished individual, always with a smile and hoping for a decent outcome, buoyed by a meeting many years back with Nelson Mandela, he believed that at some point change would come and the floodgates would open.

Madame Elysé was not awed by the Peace Palace, with its marble and gilt, stained glass and wood panels, a legacy of empire gifted by Andrew Carnegie. "I have travelled often and far," she said, with a big grin, on entering the building. "I have been to Réunion, and visited my brother in the Seychelles. I have been to the Mauritian island of Rodrigues, to learn about Chagossian cuisine. I have even been to England, to visit my children, who live there." She paused. "To tell you the truth, I did not feel so comfortable in England. The English . . . they trampled over my birthplace." Other memories were more positive. A year earlier she had been in Rome. "I travelled to the Vatican, we met the Pope, we wanted to tell others about our story." And they did, with an exhibit at the UN headquarters.

Now, after so many years, she was in The Hague, at the Court, about to enter the Great Hall of Justice, where this story began, to take a seat in the second row, behind the advocates of Mauritius. "Why did it take so long to get here?" she asked. What you have read to this point is the story I shared with her.

. . .

Sir Anerood Jugnauth opened the hearings for Mauritius, under the presidency of Judge Abdulqawi Yusuf, from Somalia, who had grown up as a child of Italian colonialism ("one of the harshest and most cruel colonial administrations anywhere in Africa," he called it). Jugnauth offered a restrained and personal narrative, the last survivor of the Lancaster House conference. "I am sorry to say that more than fifty years after independence, and more than fifty years after I travelled to London for the Constitutional Conference, the process of decolonisation of Mauritius remains incomplete as a result of the unlawful detachment of an integral part of our territory on the eve of our independence."

Four advocates for Mauritius followed in quick succession. "No country wishes to be a colony," we told the judges, drawing on Boris Johnson's recent letter of resignation as Foreign Secretary, which complained that the terms of Britain's departure from the European Union would give his country the status of a colony.

Then came Madame Elysé's moment. Twenty years on Peros Banhos, four days of forcible removal, forty-five years as a refugee in her own country, reduced to a statement of three minutes and forty-seven seconds. I introduced her from the podium, then observed the fourteen judges watch her watching herself.

"Mappel Liseby Elysé."

Unscripted, Madame Elysé spoke from the heart; she knew exactly what she wanted to say. The British Solicitor-General, Mr. Buckland, seated just a few feet away, barely looked up as she spoke, an unused pencil clutched in his hand. The Foreign Office legal adviser leaned on his left arm, apparently averting his eyes from the screen. The judges adopted postures of their own. Some leaned back in their chairs, others inclined forward, hands clasped under their chins. Some listened to the language of Creole with eyes shut, some focused on the screens, some gazed around the room.

After Madame Elysé finished, there was a long silence, as powerful as the words, then the sound of tears. The judges listened and heard, and after five decades, it was no surprise there should be emotion. The issues before the Court were not theoretical or abstract. "It concerns real people, real lives, real facts, real continuing consequences," was the best I could muster.

Our colleague Alison Macdonald comforted Madame Elysé. Later, when we spoke of the experience, she mentioned her friends, gathered in a community centre back in Port Louis, watching from afar as the proceedings were broadcast live on national television. Later, we saw a clip on Mauritian television, with its raw reactions and emotions, a mix of pride, bitterness, anger.

. . .

The British team addressed the Court that afternoon. Normally the Attorney General would have attended, but the incumbent recused himself as a friend—and pupil master—of the former Mauritian Prime Minister. Years ago, he had given legal advice in support of Mauritius's case, put it in writing, and did not support Britain's approach. So Mr. Buckland opened the case for the UK, telling the judges that his country was a strong supporter of the Court and the rule of law in international affairs, but they must reject the case. You have no jurisdiction over "a bilateral sovereignty dispute," he said. You do not have sufficient materials to reach conclusions on the key facts. It's complex, you should walk away.

As for the Chagossians, Mr. Buckland accepted on behalf of Britain that the manner of their removal—but not the fact it occurred—and subsequent treatment were "shameful and wrong." Madame Elysé's words were "very moving," and he expressed "deep respects" to the Chagossians. That was it. No commitment to right the wrongs done, no concession, nothing about allowing them to return. We paid compensation, that was amends enough. Counsel for the UK reiterated arguments raised and lost at the General Assembly, and once again made the unfortunate assertion that Mauritius was "using the Chagossians' desire to be resettled to persuade this Court to make findings on [sovereignty]." Devoid of legal merit or evidence, if the argument was intended to cause hurt, it succeeded. "I listened to the English, in the French translation," Madame Elysé said in reaction. "It did not feel good, I just heard lies."

A day in Court is long, arguments made under the large and luminous stained-glass windows, a gift from Britain during the construction of the Palace of Peace. The light illuminated the judges, but their faces offered little by way of reaction. One judge leaned back, as his neighbour adjusted her papers. A note was passed along the bench. The Italian judge coughed, then posed a question of acute significance: "What is the relevance of the will of the population of Chagossian origin?" Giorgio Gaja asked. The question, which may be the only one posed by a judge at the ICJ to feature in a novel (*Diego Garcia*, by Natasha Soobramanien and Luke Williams, May 2022), went to the core of what self-determination is about: which is the people entitled to express a view on its future? It seemed to be premised on a recognition that the views of the diaspora were not uniform, that it pulled in different directions. It was, too, a means of teasing out a commitment to ensure that the views of the Chagossians—wherever they may be in the world—must be taken into account, to determine the conditions of

Chagossian members of the delegation of Mauritius, International Court of Justice, September 2018 (including Olivier Bancoult and Liseby Elysé, *first and third from left in front row*).

a future return, and also the decisions to be taken on how life on Chagos should be organised once a return occurs.

On Tuesday morning, outside the Palace of Peace, a small group of protesters gathered in a huddle. We are Chagossians from Crawley, on the outskirts of London, they told us, but we can't get in. The British had not invited them on their delegation, nor offered them assistance to get entrance passes. Could we help?

South Africa opened the proceedings on the second morning. As a former colony, it was familiar with colonialism and forcible removals, and their long-lasting effects. "Thousands of forcibly displaced people died in concentration camps in South Africa," the advocate said to the judges, a British scorched-earth policy that caused entire communities to be taken from their homes "on the basis of race." There was no such thing as part freedom, she concluded, decolonisation is never partial. The line was Mandela's, whose bust stood outside the Great Hall.

And so it went, over three more days, as a river follows its course. Germany hoped the Court would give an opinion, but not go too far in its decision. Argentina went full throttle, driven by the Malvinas. Australia, itself a former British colony, gave a fair impression of "abused child syndrome," a victim turned perpetrator, urging the Court to rid itself of the case. Belize, Botswana and Brazil offered strong support for completing decolonisation, as did Cyprus, a member of the European Union, with its own legacy of colonial rule, home still today to unwanted British bases.

On Wednesday the US representative addressed the Court. Much had been said on the "long and difficult" process of decolonisation, the State Department legal adviser stated on behalf of Mr. Trump's administration, and on "the suffering" of the Chagossians, but offered no hint of regret as to her country's role in the story. There was no affirmation of the values President Roosevelt wrote into the Atlantic Charter, nor of Ralph Bunche's legacy, cast to the winds. The Marshall Islands and India followed, strongly supportive of Mauritius, and then Israel, with its own issues of displacement and return, appearing before the Court for the first time in decades, there to speak in support of Britain. The afternoon brought support for our side from Kenya, Nicaragua and Nigeria, and at the end of the day, the Brazilian judge asked a question that seemed encouraging, on certain effects of resolution 1514.

On the last day representatives from Serbia, Thailand and Vanuatu spoke, and then the Attorney General of Zambia addressed the Court. He was resplendent in my ill-fitting wig and gown, borrowed after he left his own outfit in Lusaka. The African Union closed the case, forcefully and elegantly. "Not a single State argued or opposed the legal principles of decolonisation and self-determination," the legal adviser told the judges. It was astounding, she declared, that so many decades on, the Court "heard a coloniser and its allies defending colonisation." She ended with a paean to the Chagossians, to Madame Elysé, who was "the voice of Africa."

THE RULING

You never can know exactly how a hearing has gone, or predict what the outcome will be. Over the years I have developed a sixth sense, one that is nourished by changes in the atmosphere in the Great Hall, by conversations with colleagues and observers, by watching the judges. We had worked intensely with our allies, meeting each evening after the day in court, to compare notes on the arguments, the gaps to be filled, the points made by opponents that needed a response. There were highs and lows and much speculation, yet the general sense was not pessimistic. The British had little support among the unattached bystanders, and the few questions from the bench did not seem hostile. But you never can tell.

A colleague prepared a note summarising what had passed. Two countries supported Britain and the United States. Forty-three lawyers had addressed the Court, including ten women, a singular improvement on the five South West Africa cases heard between 1950 and 1971, when not one of the dozens of advocates or judges was a woman. In the Chagos case, a bare majority of those who addressed the Court were white, it being addressed by advocates who were Black, Hispanic, Asian and Arab. Slowly, slowly, it might be said, the world of international law is being decolonised.

After the hearing the teams dispersed. Madame Elysé and the Chagossians took the long journey back to Port Louis, with Sir Anerood, as our counsel returned to homes in London, Washington and Montreal. You move on quickly after a hearing. As the days, weeks and months passed, I occasionally found myself wondering where the Court might end up. My Spanish mother-in-law often tells me there is never any point in worrying, as you always worry about the wrong thing. It is wise advice.

The deliberation after the hearing usually takes about six months. Over that time the judges will gather, led by the Court's President, exchanging ideas and notes, as drafts emerge and separate or dissenting opinions are written. The process is confidential. There were no leaks, no information to be interpreted or shared.

Word arrived early in the new year, informally first, from the Court's Registrar to Ambassador Koonjul, then via a press release. A public sitting would be held at 3 p.m. in The Hague, "Judge Abdulqawi Ahmed Yusuf, President of the Court, will read out the Advisory Opinion." I care about all my cases, but this one was different, going to the heart of any system of justice, how the rule of law protects the weak and vulnerable from the excesses of the powerful. In 1945, Britain and the United States had committed themselves to a rules-based international order; then they flaunted the rules. They committed themselves to Ralph Bunche's vision of decolonisation and human rights, then shredded their own commitments.

We travelled to The Hague a day ahead of the reading, to meet with the African Union and supportive countries. As with other cases, we prepared three different press releases, to deal with various eventualities: triumph, catastrophe, and something in between. The media interest was intense.

On the morning of the reading, I went for a run to the sea at nearby Scheveningen, to the pier, then to Café Clarence on Piet Heinstraat, for buttered toast, orange juice and the best coffee in The Hague. We finalised the press statements, attended meetings with allies, had a quick sandwich lunch, then took the short walk to the Court. The sun shone at the Palace of Peace, at two o'clock, in the company of Madame Elysé. "Red skirt?" I exclaimed. She nodded and smiled. "Not a sign of optimism," she said, "for this trip, I am so anxious! I think we could win or lose, but I am so anxious!" I understood, always preparing myself for the worst, steps taken to soften the bitter crush of disappointment.

Madame Elysé sat in the front row, Olivier Bancoult on one side, me on the other. A handbag nestled in her lap, she clutched her hands tightly. On my phone we watched a report from Mauritius; her friends, the ladies of Chagos, gathered before a television screen in the community centre.

The Great Hall was packed. At three o'clock, the small door to the left of us opened.

"La Cour!"

The judges trooped in, everyone stood. The fourteen slowly made their way into the room, so orderly. "Please be seated," said

Abdulqawi Yusuf, President, International Court of Justice, 2018.

President Yusuf, his eyes darting around the room. Did he make eye contact with Madame Elysé? Had he spotted Britain's Foreign Office legal adviser, tucked in a faraway corner, almost out of sight? The President sat. "The sitting is open." He read, a rhythmic incantation, his head bobbed, looking down and then up and around. At this moment in a case the sense of expectation and anxiety, excitement even, is overwhelming. "The Court meets today to deliver its advisory opinion . . . on the decolonisation of Mauritius." The name of the country was spoken so gently—as in "Now-rishus"—with a soft Somali lilt, each word neatly clipped.

A hundred or more pairs of eyes and ears scanned the Great Hall, eager for a hint of what might be to come. The reading was methodical and tantalising, as it worked its way through the various doors the Court would have to pass to reach its conclusion, a traverse across history, time and place, through the facts and into the law.

The Court had jurisdiction. Australia was swatted aside.

There were no compelling reasons to decline to exercise that jurisdiction, the Court had all the material it needed on the facts. It was for the General Assembly to decide if the questions were useful, not the Court. The issues decided by the arbitral tribunal in the basement of the Pera Palace Hotel were different, so the principle of *res judicata* did not apply. The Assembly's questions were about decolonisation, not a bilateral territorial dispute. Colonialism was a "broader frame" of reference, "inseparable" from territory, the Court could pronounce on both. "The Court cannot decline to give opinion."

The judges followed the printed text as the President spoke, peering at copies not yet available to us. They knew where this was headed, we didn't. The reading of a decision is excruciating. The Court had cast aside all jurisdictional objections. Why would it do that if it didn't want to engage with the merits? *Do not leap ahead*, I told myself. My anxieties were channelled into my left hand, which, out of sight, had slipped below the seat and clasped Madame Elysé's right hand. We held on, tightly.

President Yusuf moved on to the facts, as the Court found them, a judicial truth, not the same as *the* truth. The British and Americans had discussions, there was an "agreement," then detachment, then independence. The Chagossians left, or were "prevented from returning," or were "forcibly removed." These were strong words, "forcibly removed," not just "they left." Regret. Shame. Wrong. Compensation. A thumbprint on a sheet of paper. No return.

Then to the first question. Was decolonisation completed in accordance with the law? That depended on the content and scope of the law, on the right to self-determination after 1946, and between 1965 and 1968. The President offered a short account of history, the United Nations Charter, self-determination, Chapter XI, the legacy of Ralph Bunche, although his name wasn't mentioned. Resolution 1514 was a "defining moment," he said, one that "clarifies."

This felt increasingly hopeful. On he went. Resolution 1514 was not binding as such, of course, but it had a "normative value." It did not create a new rule, it declared an existing one; 1514 reflected a rule of customary law, one that no state voted against.

He read out paragraph six of the resolution. "Any attempt aimed at the partial or total disruption of the national unity and the territorial integrity of a country is incompatible with the purposes and principles of the Charter of the United Nations." As he spoke, I thought back to the time when those words were first drafted, wondered who typed them out, sixty years ago, passed them on to Mr. Boland, the Irish diplomat. Territorial integrity was a corollary to the right of self-determination, President Yusuf continued. The South West Africa advisory opinion of 1971 merely "consolidated" the law. Detachment by the coloniser had to be based on "the freely expressed and genuine will of the people of the territory concerned."

Was consent freely expressed and genuinely given? No, it was not. In 1965, Chagos was "clearly" an integral part of the colony. Where a part of a colony was separated to create a new colony, "heightened scrutiny" was needed on the consent of the people, all Mauritians. The spotlight settled on events in London, Harold Wilson's desire to frighten the Mauritians with hope, the meeting at Lancaster House. The detachment of Chagos "was not based on the free and genuine expression of the will of the people concerned."

I felt a squeeze of my hand. I turned to Madame Elysé, and she to me. She was not sure what it meant. I whispered, she smiled, turned back towards the President, who had concluded on the first question. There are moments when you listen and the words skip along, like the stylus of a record that loses its groove. ". . . unlawful detachment . . . a new colony . . . BIOT . . . decolonisation . . . not lawfully completed."

President Yusuf turned to the second question.

Britain's continued administration was "a wrongful act." It was unlawful when it happened, it was unlawful today. Britain must end its administration of Chagos "as rapidly as possible." Only with this would decolonisation be complete. "Its territory," the President said, speaking of Mauritius's relationship to Chagos. "*Its territory.*" "*Its territory.*" Chagos was, has always been, is a part of Mauritius, he was saying.

What was left? The Court passed the baton to the General Assembly, which must decide on the way forward. Member states would have to cooperate with the United Nations to put the modalities into effect.

And the Chagossians? The "resettlement of Mauritian nationals, including Chagossians, is an issue relating to the protection of human rights to be addressed by the General Assembly."

It took a while for the words to sink in. The deputy registrar read out the vote.

The Court was unanimous on jurisdiction.

Two judges dissented on the discretion not to exercise that jurisdiction. Just two.

Only one judge dissented on the conclusion that decolonisation was incomplete. Thirteen votes to one, in our favour. The sole dissent was the American judge.

The President spoke for sixty-four minutes. The decision was clear, the conclusion without ambiguity, widely supported by all of the judges bar one. The Court spoke in favour of Mauritius and Madame Elysé. The right to return was open. The judges stood to leave the Great Hall of Justice.

. . .

Outside the courtroom, between the busts of Mandela and Gandhi, there was ruckus and noise, as a member of the Court registry handed out printed copies of the decision. Eagerly, we parsed the pages, the individual declarations of six judges, a joint declaration by two others, the four separate opinions, the solitary dissent of the

American judge. The Court should have exercised its discretion to decline to give the opinion, she wrote, but said nothing to disagree with the merits and offered no support to the British argument. The dissent was only on jurisdiction, not the merits, and she did not follow Judge Jessup. A few days later, she and I were together at an academic conference in a faraway place. "Congratulations on the result," she said, "you must be pleased." "We are." Yes, I noticed that she said nothing about the merits.

Of the twelve judges who recorded individual views, seven mentioned the Chagossians. The forcible removal was "deplorable," the Chinese judge wrote. The British didn't even think about ascertaining their views, the French judge noted. It was regrettable that the Court did not say they should be compensated, wrote the Lebanese judge. The will of the Chagossians was significant, said the Italian judge, with or without compensation. Britain must "wipe out" the consequences of their forcible displacement, the Ugandan judge wrote. They must be able to return to their homes if they wished to do so.

Two judges evoked the words spoken by Madame Elysé. Hers was a "humanitarian tragedy" of Greek proportions, the Brazilian judge recorded. She was like Hecuba ("I, too, was prosperous once, but am so no longer; a single day robbed me of all my wealth, my happiness"). The Court should have addressed the Chagossians' right to reparations.

The Jamaican judge went further, putting Madame Elysé's words into a broader historical context. The forcible removal was akin to the abduction and enslavement of millions of Africans. Olivier Bancoult was a man of "courage and tenacity." How ironic that two centuries after her ancestors' enslavement on Peros Banhos, working on coconut plantations, she should find herself enslaved in the hull of the *Nordvaer*. How tragic that her right to return, recognised by the English court of appeal in 2001, was overturned by the vote of a single judge in the House of Lords. This was a human tragedy, one with "no place in the twenty-first century." The advances of international law after 1945, "based on respect for the inherent dignity and worth of the human person," should have prevented this wrong. How ironic that Britain was the one to make those new rules, which now must "work to the advantage of the Chagossians."

As the courtroom emptied, Madame Elysé lingered, a smile on her face. She stood next to her nephew, Olivier Bancoult. As photographs were taken, the deputy registrar came over to us.

"I saw you holding hands," he said with a smile.

"It was a big moment," I replied.

"It certainly was."

"I was surprised by the result, very surprised, my emotion is large," Madame Elysé told him. "It was the most beautiful moment," she said to me. "My testimony made the Court vibrate; I held your hand, and the judges saw it."

RETURN TO NEW YORK

The Court's ruling was widely reported. "UN Top Court" tells UK "rapidly" to end its rule of Chagos, reported *All Africa*. *Al Jazeera* and *Voice of America* ran with similar headlines. Britain's claim of sovereignty over Chagos has been rejected, declared the *Guardian*. The Indian press welcomed calls for "rapid decolonisation," as did Chinese and Russian newspapers. *The Times* of London did not mince words: "UN Court Orders Britain to Hand Over the Chagos Islands." Prime Minister Pravind Jugnauth hailed the decision as "historic." Mauritius could now "be made complete," he stated, "and when that occurs, the Chagossians and their descendants will finally be able to return home." The *New York Times* reported Ambassador Koonjul's satisfaction with the "very clear, near unanimous decision," and the prospect of "further action" at the UN.

Britain offered a muted response. Three days passed before a junior minister told Parliament that it was "an advisory opinion, not a judgement ruling." The government would read the opinion and determine how best to proceed. The following month, the Prime Ministers of Britain and Mauritius met at 10 Downing Street. Mr. Jugnauth subsequently wrote to Theresa May—the rule of law required the advisory opinion to be "promptly implemented," and Mauritius intended to table a resolution at the General Assembly. He reiterated Mauritius's strong commitment to the continuation of the US military base at Diego Garcia, and the return of the displaced Mauritians to Peros Banhos and other islands. Mauritius was willing to negotiate a treaty with the Americans, and if they wanted a role, the British could have one.

Britain decided it would not respect the advisory opinion or the rule of law. This became apparent at the end of April, when Theresa May wrote to her Mauritian counterpart, expressing regret that Chagos was referred to the Court and making it clear that Britain would, once again, ignore the judges' determinations. "Sovereignty will be ceded when the British Indian Ocean Territory is no longer needed for defence purposes," she wrote, words that might have mirrored the dismissive reaction of South Africa's government to the Court's 1971 Namibia Advisory Opinion. I ascertained that Foreign Secretary Jeremy Hunt had been presented with two options—Britain could sit down with the Mauritians and Americans and work out a sensible arrangement on the basis of the law, or it could dig in its heels and tough it out on national security grounds. Mr. Hunt opted for the second option: the Court had erred, Britain would hang on and, he warned, further recourse to the UN would be "a big irritant."

This position was duly made public. "The United Kingdom respects the ICJ," a minister told the House of Commons, but not enough to give effect to the opinion, which was merely advisory. "We do not share the Court's approach." The leader of the opposition Labour Party expressed concern at the disregard of international law. "To go against the Advisory Opinion will set the UK against the entire continent of Africa and dozens of other countries," he wrote, and committed his party to respect the Court's decision "in full," and to "ensure that Chagossians are able to return to their homes."

Britain's reaction strengthened the resolve to move forward at the UN. Ambassador Koonjul consulted with the African group and other countries, and we were asked to prepare a draft resolution. As Britain lobbied actively, with support from the United States, its new permanent representative, Karen Pierce, rehashed the same arguments that had already been twice rejected, first by the General Assembly, then by the Court. No doubt about sovereignty, bilateral dispute, and so on. Urging countries to vote against the resolution, she must have recognised the weakness of the arguments, given the clarity with which the Court had spoken. In bilateral conversations, she made other arguments, some of which were surprising. "We need to stay in control for reasons of security, ours and yours," she explained to Ambassador Koonjul. "What if we are attacked by aliens?"

"Surely she spoke in jest?" I suggested to the ambassador, when he mentioned this.

"Believe me it was not in jest," he replied instantly. "She was dead serious!"

Senegal circulated the draft resolution, a preamble with eight operative paragraphs to welcome the Court's opinion, affirm Chagos as "an integral part" of Mauritius, and call for the resettlement of the Chagossians "as a matter of urgency." Britain must "withdraw its colonial administration" within six months, and "pose no impediment" to the return of the former inhabitants. Member states, the UN and its specialised agencies, and all other international organisations, must recognise Chagos as part of Mauritius, and ignore all measures purportedly taken on behalf of the "British Indian Ocean Territory."

On 22 May 2019, Senegal and Venezuela opened the debate, speaking for the African group and the Non-Aligned Movement. Prime Minister Jugnauth was the third to speak. To vote against the resolution would be to endorse colonialism, he said, adding that the forcible eviction of the Chagossians was "akin to a crime against humanity." This was the first occasion a Mauritian leader levelled the charge, carefully formulated on the basis of the Court's language of "forcible removal" of the Chagossians, words that chimed with the ICC Statute's reference to "forcible deportation" as a "crime against humanity."

Urging a vote against, the British ambassador invoked Chagos's vital role on humanitarian relief, maritime search and rescue and security, passing in silence on Diego Garcia's role in extraordinary rendition and the Iraq war. Britain had no doubt about its sovereignty—but did she? many will have wondered—and considered the detachment to have been agreed, despite the Court's finding to the contrary. It was as though the British ambassador had not read the ruling. There was more regret, on the "manner" of the Chagossians' removal, but not the fact it occurred, nor Britain's desire to keep them out. Britain wanted to improve their lives, with money, and perhaps a brief visit to their former homes. But to be able to return? No way. They could have "heritage visits," but nothing more. And, the ambassador made clear, she was particularly displeased with the reference to "crimes against humanity." "Serious allegation . . . gross mischaracterisation . . . hope it won't be repeated," she warned. Listening to her, I was reminded of when I was six years old, scolded by my headmistress, Mrs. Brewster, who wore brown sandals even in winter and was married to Colonel Brewster, who had a big moustache and, we were told, had fought in the Boer War.

Two countries spoke in support of Britain: the United States, with an interest of its own, and the Maldives, for reasons entirely unclear. Over many years, Mauritius had sought to negotiate a maritime boundary with its Indian Ocean neighbour, but the newly appointed permanent representative of the Maldives raised unfathomable concerns that the resolution might create ambiguity about her country's maritime rights.

A string of countries spoke in favour of the resolution, motivated no doubt by anti-colonial instincts, some with barely concealed skeletons of their own. Nicaragua and Syria, then Argentina, keen to draw a link with the Malvinas and Falklands. Cyprus hoping for "a move away from the colonial paradigm," Mexico and Uruguay opting for the rule of law. Namibia hoped for an end to colonialism, South Africa wanted an end to a world that "considered some peoples more worthy than others." Egypt, Botswana, Lesotho, Zimbabwe, Madagascar leaned in, and the Seychelles made the point that "picking and choosing" the advisory opinions you supported—a sort of *à la carte* international law—was not an option.

India closed the debate, with the authority of a former colony that had first-hand experience of Britain's largesse, a coloniser that liked to "divide and rule," leaving trails of mayhem and turmoil. The Indian ambassador spoke with sadness as he swatted away each of the British ambassador's points. A bilateral dispute? No. Consent circumvented? No. Security concerns? No.

The sound of power shifting was reflected in the vote, as the board turned an even brighter shade of green than two years earlier. There were now just four islets of dissent, blinking red in support of London and Washington: Hungary, Israel, the Maldives and Australia. Those supporting resolution 73/295 grew to 116, including Ireland and several other European Union members. What would Dr. Bunche and Mr. Boland have made of it all, I wondered, as the screen went green.

"Embarrassing," the *New York Times* would report. As journalists sharpened their pencils, the British ambassador picked up the shards, delivering a statement to explain her country's vote.

Depleted and crumpled, eyes watery, she held a sheaf of papers but, bereft of decent words, dissembled. Britain is firmly committed to self-determination, she declared, in response to Argentina's reference to the Falklands, but there would be no dialogue on sovereignty until the Falkland islanders so wished. As the implications of her words sank in, it was hard not to feel a moment of empathy for a distinguished diplomat placed by her government in so awkward a situation. One rule for the white Falklanders, another for the Black Chagossians, that was what many heard her to be saying.

Mural, Chagos Refugee Group
Resource Centre, Port Louis, 2021.

Epilogue: *Bleu de Nîmes*

———◆———

"Peros vert, peros vert, so pep noir,
nu pep noir, nu pep noir
noune déraciné"

—TON VIÉ, 2008

We are twenty-five on the dock of Mahé port, looking across the Indian Ocean. Led by Ambassador Koonjul, the group includes marine scientists, journalists, lawyers and academics from eight different countries, and five Chagossians, the largest cohort. Liseby Elysé is here with Olivier Bancoult, her nephew, and three other colleagues: Marcel Humbert, her childhood friend from Île du Coin; Rosemonde Berthin, who spent the first seventeen years of her life on the Salomon islands; and Suzelle Baptiste, removed from Diego Garcia as an eleven-month-old "contract labourer." Of the five, only Marcel was not in The Hague for the hearings.

We have come to the Seychelles to travel to Chagos on the *Bleu de Nîmes*, a converted Royal Navy minesweeper, a thousand miles to the east. The journey will take five days, and even more to return. (We hoped to leave from the Maldives, but the government refused permission; departing from Rodrigues in Mauritius was thwarted by a tropical cyclone.)

In Chagos we will carry out a scientific survey of Blenheim Reef to see whether any part of it is a drying reef, one that is partly above the sea. The information will be used to determine the line of the future maritime boundary between Chagos and the Maldives. We will visit Salomon, ten miles to the west of Blenheim, and Peros Banhos, another thirty miles further west. The journey will be historic: the first visit organised by Mauritius; the first return by Chagossians without a British escort; the first involving British journalists. And it will be my first visit, a decade or more after being contacted by Mauritius and being told by Britain and the United

States that recourse to international law and courts to end the last British colony in Africa was "hopeless."

. . .

As we prepare to depart, three years have passed since the Court in The Hague ruled that Chagos was part of the territory of Mauritius, and that Britain must end its illegal occupation. The UN General Assembly had resolved that it must leave by the end of 2019, but the date has come and gone, ignored by Britain. London has dug in its heels, issuing a stream of diplomatic notes, press statements and answers to parliamentary questions that invariably open with the same words:

> "The United Kingdom has no doubt about its sovereignty over the Chagos Archipelago, which has been under continuous British sovereignty since 1814. Mauritius has never held sovereignty over the Archipelago and we do not recognize its claim."

The absence of doubt is striking, since the British have been unable to persuade any international judge—not even one—to express support for its claim to the archipelago. This raises serious questions about the country's purported commitment to the rule of law. Two Prime Ministers and five Foreign Secretaries have embraced lawlessness, for reasons that are unclear, hoping to tough it out and make the problem go away.

It won't, because those most directly affected by Britain's continuing obstinacy won't allow it to. This is apparent when I visit Crawley, near Gatwick Airport, to spend time with Chagossian exiles living in Britain. The ICJ ruling offers the prospect of a return, while generating a raft of different views. Some worry that publicity about their mistreatment, and its racial element, may cause a backlash. Others are concerned about housing and jobs, or being deported from Britain, because not all have the right to British nationality. Others are anxious that a return to Chagos might mean rules being imposed from Port Louis, without any real autonomy. A few hope that Chagos might even become an independent country, even if they recognise that its size and location, and international law's recognition that the archipelago is part of Mauritius, make that unlikely.

"We want some autonomy," Joseph Bertrand explains, "so we can decide for ourselves what happens on our territory, our environment and our culture." They want a dedicated member of parliament in Port Louis, like Rodrigues (the island has autonomous status in Mauritius, with a regional assembly and executive council). They are right to be cautious and careful, given past and continuing mistreatments, and to insist that they be fully involved in decision-making that touches on the future of the land of their birth.

There are many views in the Chagossian diaspora, often expressed with passion and energy. But one perspective shared by all is a deep commitment to the right of return, if they wish, whether to Peros Banhos or Salomon, or any other island, including Diego Garcia. "Why should Filipinos, Bangladeshis and Mauritians work at the military base with the Americans, but not us?" It's a fair question.

"How many of you will actually want to return?" I ask.

"All of us," they reply. "The ICJ has ruled, we have the right to live there, we will never give up."

The Chagossians I spend time with in Mauritius express the same sentiment. Suzelle Baptiste shows me around the Chagos Refugee Group's centre, on the walls of which hang portraits of those who passed away before their dreams of a return could be fulfilled. The bright and colourful building, with its many hopeful murals, hosts a modest, affecting museum. The collection includes a wooden trunk, like the one Liseby carried when she left Peros Banhos, lined with the pages of an old English newspaper from the 1950s, and other curiosities; a tool to hulk coconuts, an old iron, a hoe, a tambourine, many seashells and a small bowl filled with the finest white sand I have ever touched, from Peros Banhos. Here too is Olivier Bancoult's office, with many photographs decorating its walls: Olivier with Nelson Mandela ("The struggle goes on!" the South African President told him); with Pope John Paul II; with many Chagossians waiting on the dock in Port Louis to make a British-run "heritage visit" to Chagos in 2006.

At Liseby's home in Port Louis I have lunch with family and friends; octopus stew, a rich Peros Banhos speciality, served with Eureka red, a local wine. The ICJ and UN determinations have sharpened her optimism and resolve. She lights up, recalling the hearings in the Great Hall, watching the judges enter, led by the President, a Black man from Africa.

"He looked me in the eye on that first day," she says. "I thought: 'Maybe he will do something for us.' I felt something."

And on the day of judgement?

"As we sat down, he looked at me again, in the eye, directly, and the way he looked, I thought: 'It will be all right.'"

The memory brings another smile, and a question.

"Will London change its mind?"

Yes, but not quite yet. Digging in your heels means business as usual until a face-saving opportunity arises.

A Bahraini-owned telecommunications company called Sure continues to offer telephone and internet services in the Chagos area. (Without a licence from Port Louis, its services are illegal under Mauritian law.)

Sportsbet.io, a betting company, and many other companies, maintain their use of the .io domain name, assigned to the "British Indian Ocean Territory" with the support of Britain, but without Mauritian authorisation. The British government denies that it receives financial benefit.

The Pobjoy Mint, a family concern in southern England, still issues "BIOT" currency. Last year it brought out a shiny new fifty-pence coin, the Chagos anemonefish (clownfish) on one side, the Queen on the other.

The renowned Zoological Society of London (Patron: HM The

Queen) publicises its marine conservation activities in Chagos and future expeditions to "one of the most amazing marine environments anywhere in the world." The chief executive happens to be a former British diplomat.

MRAG, a modest British company, contributes to the management of the illegal Chagos marine protected area, under a British government contract. Its chairman happens to be a former chief scientist to the British government. He is also president of the ZSL.

Viewed from London, these and other activities in Chagos are seen as lawful and profitable. Yet the refusal to recognise Mauritian sovereignty, or support the return of the Chagossians, comes at a price: Britain's reputation as a guardian of the international rule of law is shattered. With increasing frequency and force, the charge of "crime against humanity" is levelled, for the forcible deportation of the 1960s, for today's refusal to facilitate a return. The charge rankles the Foreign Office, which complains with diplomatic *notes verbales* and comments from its High Commissioner in Port Louis. Yet there is support for the charge: a recent decision of judges in The Hague authorises the International Criminal Court Prosecutor to investigate Myanmar's refusal to allow the Rohingya to return from Bangladesh to their homes on the basis that it may be a "crime against humanity."

And Britain's international support for its claim to the Chagos Archipelago is limited to a tiny handful of countries: Hungary, Israel, the Maldives and Australia—with its modest military contingent on Diego Garcia, and a post office—and the United States, although that country's position seems increasingly untenable. President Joe Biden's assertion that respect for the rule of law is one of his country's "most cherished democratic values"—a stick with which to beat Russia (for its occupation of Crimea and war against Ukraine) and China (for failing to respect an international ruling on its illegal activities in the South China Seas)—rings hollow. The "do nothing" stance allows these countries to swat away any attack: What about Chagos? One rule for you, another for us?

British Indian Ocean Territory stamp, 2021.

As Britain complains about Russia's illegal occupation of Ukraine, it continues to illegally occupy a part of Africa.

For its part, the UN is implementing the advisory opinion. An early step was to change its map of the world, which now shows Chagos as an undisputed part of Mauritius.

The Food and Agriculture Organisation, a UN specialised agency, declined to register Britain's acceptance of a fisheries treaty premised on its claimed sovereignty over Chagos.

The Universal Postal Union, another specialised agency, banned the use of postage stamps issued by "the territory formerly known as the 'British Indian Ocean Territory.'" The one issued last year, of a royal angelfish and the Queen, is unusable, a collector's item.

Other UN bodies will follow. So will other governments and international organisations. It is a matter of time, I say to Liseby, just as it was for South Africa in its illegal occupation of Namibia.

Courts too are taking their cue from the ICJ. After its vote against the UN resolution on the advisory opinion, Mauritius invited the Maldives to delimit the maritime boundary with Chagos. When the Maldives refused, taking refuge in Britain's claim, Mauritius sued it at the ITLOS in Hamburg. The Maldives asked the Tribunal to rule that it could not exercise jurisdiction, as doing so would require it to rule on the rights of an indispensable third state that was not a party to the case. This is known as the *Monetary Gold* principle, in honour of an ICJ ruling from the 1950s. ITLOS rejected the argument: the principle did not apply, as the UK had no rights or claim to Chagos and was not an indispensable party, as the determinations of the ICJ were "authoritative" and had "legal effect," a conclusion strengthened by Britain's failure to leave by the date imposed by the UN General Assembly. As I write, the case proceeds before ITLOS, which will delimit the maritime boundary. Shortly, the Maldives will share a delimited southern boundary with Mauritius and Africa, not Britain.

London's response to the ruling is pure *Alice in Wonderland.* The ITLOS judgement had "no effect" for Britain, a minister informed Parliament, which was free to negotiate a maritime boundary of its own, between "BIOT" and the Maldives.

"What is to be done?" Madame Elysé asks during our lunch, seated on a sofa in her deliciously pink living room, replete with family photographs and a portrait of the Queen, for whom she has a soft spot.

"Britain will recognise the legal and political realities," I say. "Mauritius will exercise its sovereignty." My hope is that the two countries will enter into a long-term strategic relationship, one that maintains the US base at Diego Garcia, and allows the Chagossians to return. "You will be able to go back to Peros Banhos, one day."

"I feel a *chagrin,* but continue to have hope." She pauses. "The English? It hurts that they have treated us as they do, that they continue to cause us to suffer." Ever pragmatic and decent, she doesn't see why they would not now wish to help her return.

"One day we will go there together, I promise."

"Ahhh," she sighs. "Ahhh. That would be nice, really nice."

. . .

Just a few weeks later, the day before Christmas, I telephone Liseby, to share the news that we will soon be able to travel together to Peros Banhos.

"I am excited," she says, "and emotional."

The trip has been made possible by the case against the Maldives in Hamburg, and an issue about Blenheim Reef, whether and how often any part of it is above water. Mauritius has told the UK that it will carry out a scientific survey of the reef, and its connection to the Salomon islands. This will generate information to assist ITLOS in the delimitation of the boundary. Invited to confirm that it will not impede the survey—and face more legal proceedings if it fails to do so—London blinks. It says it will not impede the survey.

The protection offered by the ITLOS proceedings allowed Liseby, her four Chagossian colleagues and me to meet on the dock in Mahé, to board together the *Bleu de Nîmes*. Three days out, we celebrate our passage into the waters of Mauritius, the exclusive economic zone that extends 200 nautical miles west of Peros Banhos. Mysteriously, it is around here that the ship loses its internet connection, cutting the passengers' communication with the outside world. Captain Mascia Poma—one of the world's few female maritime captains—tells us this has never happened before. Fortunately, the journalists have satellite phones and a separate dish allowing broadcasts.

The following day, about eight miles from Peros Banhos, Liseby peers through binoculars to see her birthplace, the sandy fringe and palm trees of Île du Coin, the reef with its breaking waves. The proximity of land brings birds: lesser frigates, petrels, skuas, terns and an albatross.

Captain Poma guides the boat slowly through the narrow passage that separates Île Poule and Île Petite Soeur, into a pristine lagoon revealing different shades of blue, encircled by a fringe of deep-green islands and islets. It is difficult to overstate the enormity or beauty of what we are seeing, an ecosystem in its glorious, natural state, as it was in 1837, on the chart prepared by the British Admiralty. The anchor is lowered, two cables from the beach; Liseby stands on an upper deck pointing to the spot where her house was. Her smile is large, her eyes dance. Two smaller boats are lowered and I join the journalists on the first one out, to film the return of the Chagossians, on an amphibious landing craft, a modest version of the ones used in the D-Day landings on Normandy, a navigator standing at the bow directing the craft's way around the rocks and coral reefs that lie on the sandy bed of the lagoon. We pull up by the remains of the long, old jetty, the rusted, broken rails visible, the wheels of the little carts lying under the water. Olivier is the first off, and he sinks to his knees; Liseby bends down to clutch a handful of sand, which trickles through her fingers. The five stand together in prayer, holding hands. I confess that I cry.

There is work to be done. Due to erosion, a stone plaque marking the 2006 visit is hauled to higher land. Then we're off to see the old buildings, past the wells that confirm the availability of fresh water, through the dense, rich, humid growth, around the sprouting coconut plants and huge fallen leaves. We spend a while in the small church where Liseby, Marcel and Olivier were baptised, throwing out old coconuts and dried palm leaves, hacking away the growth to reveal the curve of the nave; the church walls are strong, yellow and green with tropical mould. Across the way is the administrator's house, easily recognisable from the old photograph I have brought with me, from the two stone pillars that marked the entrance and the eighteen steps of the stone staircase that once led to the first floor.

The wooden upper floor has disappeared, consumed by the building, along with the bright red corrugated-iron roof, now a heap of rust. Behind the house is an outbuilding, the concrete toilet seat preserved and serving as the roof to the

Peros Banhos, February 2022.

home of a large, defensive and irritated coconut crab. The roots of a huge banyan tree have overwhelmed the stone steps, surrounded by five decades of debris—decaying beams, iron fences, old coconuts and dried palm leaves. Nature has crushed colonial civilisation.

The next day, we visit Île de Baddam, part of Salomon, where Rosemonde was born in 1954. She guides us through the palm jungle to the many buildings that remain, although none has a roof: the forge, where the blacksmith worked; the church, built in 1935, where she was baptised, with one wooden window frame left in place, two stained-glass panes, bright green; the prison, with three cells. The tour continues, to the remains of the children's crèche and the very room in the hospital where she gave birth to her first child, William, in 1972, just before she was forcibly removed. Later, after a brief downpour, in the cemetery we find the gravestone of Madame Yvon Dyson, née Denise Rose, who died on 14 March 1955, aged twenty-seven. "She was the midwife who brought me into the world," Rosemonde says, but Madame Yvon died not long after, in childbirth. Nearby, the grave of Madame William Macintyre, née Rachel Chauvin, wife of the island's administrator, who died in 1923. Further along rests Dookie, who departed this world in March 1880.

Later, we come across an old metal sign, painted white with a red rim. Signed by the "BIOT Commissioner's representative," it warns trespassers of criminal prosecution. The sign is hauled down, memento of a bygone age, maybe to end up in a museum. Before we leave, there is an impromptu ceremony, to recall the memory of the ancestors, in which the Mauritian flag is raised on the old flagstaff at the end of the remains of the pier.

On the third day we return to Île du Coin. Another plaque is laid, a flag raised, an impromptu ceremony held, words shared with each other. It's amazing, I say, that but for three international tribunals and the rulings of a couple of dozen judges on matters of international law, we would not be here on Peros Banhos. Lunch on the beach follows, as Marcel and Rocco, an Italian crew member, hunt crabs. Liseby perches on the long, thin, sturdy trunk of

Liseby Elysé, Peros Banhos, February 2022, points to the location of her former home.

an ancient palm that has fallen across the sand and hangs over the blue water. She bounces up and down, laughing. "Like when I lived here," she says.

She will dance gently on the sand, for hours, to the amplified beat of her favourite songs, "Peros Vert" and "Grand Maman Chagossien," in harmony with Olivier, Marcel, Suzelle and Rosemonde, the tightest of tight groups. In the afternoon, we head off on one of the small boats to find and clean up the cemetery at the end of the island, just a kilometre long and a few hundred metres wide. The space is tranquil, a rare spot in which the palms have not invaded, as though out of respect. The gravestones date back to the nineteenth century and beyond, bounded by the remains of a low stone wall, separated from the beach by a row of palms. Most names have been washed away by time and moisture. Olivier finds the grave of his grandfather, Alfred Elysé, who was Liseby's father-in-law and who taught Marcel to fish. The three clean the grave, lay fresh flowers, and install a small black metal cross.

The cemetery offers a sense of order, of community and longevity. It is a place of memory and imagination, one that underscores the awfulness of the Foreign Office lawyer's advice that Britain could do as it wished, since Liseby and the other inhabitants were mere transients, people who didn't truly "belong" on Chagos. Nothing beats being in a place to be able to grasp the true scale of an act of appalling wrongdoing.

Our fourth day is largely spent around Blenheim Reef. We have by now noted that two ships have been tailing us for three days, rather obviously, but have turned off their lights and automatic identification system (AIS). But late in the night an alert crew member spots that one ship has briefly switched on its AIS, which identifies it as the *Grampian Frontier*, a British-flagged ship leased to the "BIOT" administration.

Captain Poma calls the ship, and, after an exchange of greetings and locations, asks: "What is your purpose in the Chagos?"

The VHF radio crackles, then an Irish (or maybe Northern Irish) male voice answers:

"*Bleu de Nîmes*, this is *Grampian Frontier*, we are conducting fisheries patrols in the area."

"Thank you, have a good watch, Captain."

"All copied, Ma'am, standing by, out."

The short exchange is interesting. There are no other ships over an area of hundreds of square miles, and we are quite obviously not engaged in illicit fishing. Britain has no right under international law to patrol fishing activities in the territorial waters of Mauritius, which these are. And, as Captain Poma astutely notes, as one of a handful of female captains around the world, she is always referred to as "Captain" or "Sir," never as "Ma'am."

"They know exactly who we are and what we are doing!" she says, mischievously. "It's a chess game."

The trip concludes with a third and final visit to Blenheim Reef. It is vast, a lagoon inside the crater's rim of a long-extinct volcano, covering an area twice the size of the City of Westminster in London. We have previously spotted a couple of whales and numerous sharks, and Marcel has tantalised us with his artisanal-style fishing from the back of the boat, having snared a tuna, a grouper and several red snappers. Yet nothing beats the exhilaration, as we circumnavigate Blenheim, of the ten dolphins that dance in and out of the water, playing with us and our small boat.

Inside the reef's lagoon, the Swedish and Mauritian scientists have placed Instruments to measure the depth of the sea over time, the rise and fall of the tides. They have identified many small rocks that peek above the water at various times of the day, and flown two drones over the entire area, to produce a three-dimensional map. They are searching for the highest points on the reef, and for signs of any part of it that dries out, which may entitle Mauritius to more sea. This we find on our last morning, to considerable excitement, a decent stretch of sand, pockmarked with small rocks. It is 6:30 a.m.

"We should put a flag on it!" suggests Ola Oskarsson, the Swedish marine expert who is leading the scientific expedition.

"Good idea," Ambassador Koonjul concurs. Ten minutes later, Ola and Tomas are back in their white overalls, joined by Rezah— three scientists, in the little red dinghy heading across the reef to the patch of sand. The marine surveyors will record the location with precise instruments, raise another flag, sing the anthem of Mauritius, take photographs. These are, we believe, the first ones ever to be taken of this extraordinary, briefly drying speck of Indian Ocean reef.

"A revelation," Ola calls it, in keeping with his dude-like style.

It is a fine way to end our five days in Chagos, to be followed by six more on a rougher sea that slows our return to the Seychelles. The journey has given the lie to the notions that the islands had no permanent population in the 1960s, or that they are uninhabitable today. In the company of Marcel, we would all do just fine on any of these islands, and would do a far better job than Britain in preserving the historic buildings and cemeteries and keeping the islands free of the plastic and other rubbish and debris that abounds in Chagos today.

I find it hard to repress the sense of fury at the wrongs that have been done here. Yet Liseby is as stoical as ever. Sitting on the deck of the boat, with Marcel, they reminisce about childhood, hide-and-seek amid the palms, playing mummies and daddies.

"Marcel was just the same back then. Busy, busy, busy!" she says.

"And Liseby?" I ask.

Marcel offers a magical, mellow grin, one that suffuses every aspect of his face.

"Same. Round, round, round."

He stands up, puffs out his body, stoops to shorten himself, and waddle-bounces away.

We roar with laughter. He presses his fingers on Liseby's fore-head, a lifetime of affection.

"Can I ask one thing?" Marcel says.

"Of course."

"As we pass Île Poule, could we stop, just for an hour, so I can fish?"

"Yes," says Liseby. "A good idea. I can sit with you. That will be nice."

Liseby Elysé, Peros Banhos, 12 February 2022.

Postscript

In November 2022, a few weeks after this book was published in the UK, the British government announced that it had decided to enter into negotiations with Mauritius on the exercise of sovereignty over the Chagos Archipelago.

The announcement, which was unexpected, followed a meeting in New York between the prime ministers of the two countries, a few weeks earlier. They agreed that negotiations should secure an agreement "on the basis of international law" and take into account the ruling of the ICJ, the beating heart of this book.

As negotiations were underway, Human Rights Watch published a report on Chagos. This concluded that the forced deportations of Liseby Elysé and other Chagossians were "crimes against humanity that continue to the present," the first time the organisation had laid such a charge against the United States.

Human Rights Watch called for the Chagossians to be allowed to return, for Britain and the United States to make reparations, and for accountability of those responsible for the crimes.

It seems there may be grounds for optimism. The decolonisation of Mauritius could soon be completed, respect for the rule of law restored. The aspirations of Liseby Elysé, who told the judges of the International Court of her desire to return to the place of her birth, might be fulfilled.

I saw her a few weeks ago, in Port Louis. We talked and we danced. "I will return," she said, with a new sense of assurance, and a smile that warmed the whole of my heart.

"A civilisation that plays fast and loose with its principles is a dying civilisation."

—AIMÉ CÉSAIRE, *Discours sur le colonialisme*, 1955
(*Discourse on Colonialism*, trans. 2000)

Acknowledgements

In writing this book I have benefited from the ideas and input of a great number of colleagues and friends over the years, to whom I express my deep gratitude, while making clear that responsibility for any error or infelicity is mine alone.

It has been a privilege to come to know so many members of the remarkable Chagossian communities in Mauritius and London, so generous and open. Liseby Elysé and Olivier Bancoult are remarkable and courageous individuals, and they and their families have taught me much about patience, dignity and courage. My thanks too to Gianny Steven Augustin, Jessica Bancoult, Marilyne Bancoult, Aaron Salomon Bancoult Veerabadren, Evelyna Bancoult Veerabadren, Eliane Baptiste, Suzelle Baptiste, Rosemonde Berthin, Joseph Silvy Bertrand, Bashir Ebrahimkhan, Billy Winsley Furcy, Marie Mimose Furcy, Janine Sadrien and Rosemond Samynaden.

My connection with Chagos is the consequence of a professional engagement, and I am indebted to Navin Ramgoolam, the late Sir Anerood Jugnauth and Pravind Jugnauth for placing their trust in me. Their leadership, and the support of their teams, has been inspirational. Mauritius and its people are fortunate to have the support of public servants of the very highest quality, and it has been a privilege and a happiness to work with so many, in Port Louis and beyond: special thanks to Nayen Ballah, Dheeren Dabee, Jagdish Koonjul, Milan Meeterbhan, Aruna Devi Narain, Rajesh Ramloll, Sateeaved Seeballuck, Suresh Seeballuck and Martine Young Kim Fat.

Originally catalysed by an invitation to deliver a set of lectures, I thank the President and members of the Curatorium of the Hague Academy of International Law, and its Secretary-General, Marc Thouvenin, and staff, for offering me that opportunity.

Our legal team—from London to Washington, from Delhi to Montreal—has been more or less constant over the years. Special thanks to Paul Reichler, for his leadership and collegiality, and to Remi Reichhold for a commitment that goes well beyond the call of duty of friendship. Thanks too to Matt Craven, Pierre d'Argent, Douglas Guilfoyle, Christina Hioureas, Ruth Kennedy, Sydney Kentridge, Pierre Klein, Andrew Loewenstein, Alison Macdonald, Sean Murphy, Yuri Parkhomenko and Anjolie Singh; and to Nancy Lopez for administrative support; Scott Edmonds, Alex Tait and Vickie Taylor for cartography; and Paul Venables at Matrix Chambers for endless support.

Many other lawyers have contributed to the stories told in this book: thanks to Dapo Aklande, Carlos Arguello, Caleb Christopher, Shotaro Hamamoto, Ben Juratowich, Likando Kalaluka, Marcelo Kohen, Robert McCorquodale, Pauline Mcharo, Alina Miron, Namira Negm and Jennifer Robinson, and also to the memory of Dewa Mavhinga, of Human Rights Watch. My appreciation too for the many distinguished opponents along the way, who have, by their roles, contributed to the idea of the rule of law.

Beyond The Hague, my thanks to Arshan Barzani, Daniel Bethlehem, Douglas Blausten, Owen Bowcott, Alan Boyle, Ian Brunskill, Richard Burt, Fran Burwell, James Cameron, Sara Collins, Jeremy Corbyn MP, Duncan Currie, Elizabeth de Santo, Agnès Desarthe, Richard Dunne, Adriana Fabra, Richard Gifford, Andrew Harding, Afua Hirsch, Ben Jaffey, Andrew Jampoler, Peter Jones, Iain Macleod, Sindiwe Magona, Diana Matar, Hisham Matar, the late Thomas Mensah, Andrew Mitchell MP, Cullen Murphy, Lisa Nandy MP, Sandeep Parmar, Nigel Pleming, Andrew Sanger, Haroon Siddique, Gerry Simpson, David Snoxell (and the Chagos Islands [British Indian Ocean Territory] All-Party Parliamentary Group), Nick Timothy, Peter Tomka, Tom Tugendhat MP, David Vine, Michael Waibel, Nigel Wenban-Smith and Abdulqawi Yusuf. Thanks too to all my colleagues at the Law Faculty at University College London for their support and forbearance, led by Dean Piet Eekhout, and all colleagues and staff at Matrix Chambers.

In London, Luis Viveros Montoya has offered exceptional research assistance over so many years. To work on the audio version with Adjoah Andoh has been a wonderful experience.

On the *Bleu de Nîmes*, on the trip to Chagos, my deep gratitude to Captain Mascia Poma and her wonderful crew, in particular Oguz Aybec, Michele Celentano, Giorgio Mercenaro, Ozan Degirmeci, Rocco Zullino and chef Luca Strafella; and to all our fellow travellers, not least Rezah Badal, Ed Habershon, Ola Oskarsson, Tomas Mennerdahl, Stuart Phillips and Bruno Rinvolucri.

Jenny Lord, my editor at Weidenfeld & Nicolson, has offered constant, intelligent and minute support, along with my copyeditor Richard Mason, Georgia Goodall, Cait Davies, Katie Espiner and Maura Wilding. At Alfred Knopf, I feel blessed to work with Vicky Wilson. My agents Georgia Garrett and Melanie Jackson are more than any writer could hope for.

At home, not a day goes by in which I do not thank my lucky stars for sharing a life with Natalia Schiffrin, who holds my feet to the ground, reads every word, and offers a constant, critical, vital and wonderful presence. My gratitude too to the family—my parents, children and brother—for their love and support.

To conclude, I express the deepest gratitude to the two individuals to whom this book is dedicated, both of whom died in the past months, having offered to me half a lifetime of collegiality and love, with never a cross word.

Over thirty years, Louise Rands Silva has transcribed every interview I have ever conducted; typed and corrected each manuscript I have written; and offered ideas and reaction to characters and themes, always enriching my perceptions. To have had the benefit of such substantive input is beyond measure; that it should have been accompanied by warmth, intelligence, humour and generosity of spirit is a blessing. I value the journey we have taken together more than words could ever express.

For even longer, James Crawford, with his special Australian spirit, has been so generous in offering a unique friendship and intellectual and professional leadership. Since we first met in 1987, he has taught me about independence, integrity and principle, the courage to take on the causes you care about, and what it means to work as part of a team. It was James who offered me a first chance to work before the International Court of Justice, and but for him I doubt the opportunity to work on Chagos and self-determination would have come my way. In many ways, the stories told in this book, and the legal outcome, are a part of his extraordinary legacy.

I shall miss you both very much.

Notes

13 "The modern world has come to the realisation": Brian Urquhart, *Ralph Bunche: An American Odyssey* (W.W. Norton & Company, 1998), 115.

14 "most far-reaching declaration": *Ibid.*, 121.

14 Bunche recognised the limits: Ralph Bunche, "Trusteeship and Non-Self-Governing Territories in the Charter of the United Nations," *Department of State Bulletin*, 13 (1945), 1025 at 1037.

14 The origins of Chapter XI: John Stuart Mill, *Considerations on Representative Government* (Parker & Bourne, 1861).

14 Such ideas prompted Vladimir Ilyich Lenin: V.I. Lenin, *Lenin Collected Works*, vol. 20 (Progress Publishers, 1972), 393–454.

14 One of his Fourteen Points: "President Woodrow Wilson's Speech to the US Congress, 'Fourteen Points' (Transcript)" (8 January 1918) <https://millercenter.org/the-presidency/presidential-speeches/january-8-1918-wilsons-fourteen-points>.

15 "right of self-determination": Arnulf Becker Lorca, "Petitioning the International: A 'Pre-History' of Self-Determination," *European Journal of International Law*, 25 (2014), 497, at 499.

15 They threatened British control: "The Atlantic Conference & Charter, 1941 (Milestones: 1937–45)" (Office of the Historian, US Department of State) <https://history.state.gov/milestones/1937-1945/atlantic-conf> accessed 25 October 2019.

15 a "highly charged" quarrel: Theodore A. Wilson, *The First Summit: Roosevelt and Churchill at Placentia Bay 1941* (Macdonald, 1969), 122.

16 Roosevelt hoped to replace: *Ibid.*, 13.

16 A statement of intentions: "The Talk of the Town" [1944], *The New Yorker*, 19.

16 "their own nation-state": Stefan Oeter, "Self-Determination," B. Simma, D.E. Khan, G. Nolte, and A. Paulus (eds), *The Charter of the United Nations: A Commentary*, 3rd edn (Kindle, Oxford University Press, 2012), para 5.

17 No, he assured the House of Commons: *Ibid.*

17 Those who owed allegiance: HC Deb 9 September 1941, Vol 374, col 69 (Hansard).

17 Across Africa, many read: Bonny Ibhawoh, "Testing the Atlantic Charter: Linking Anticolonialism, Self-Determination and Universal Human Rights," *International Journal of Human Rights*, 18 (2014), 842.

17 a commitment for the "Africanization": Bonny Ibhawoh, *Human Rights in Africa* (Cambridge University Press, 2018), 130–31 (citing the UK National

Archives CO 554/133/3, Memorandum on the Atlantic Charter and British West Africa by the West African Press Delegation to the United Kingdom, 1 August 1943).

17 In South Africa, a young Nelson Mandela: Nelson Mandela, *Long Walk to Freedom* (Abacus, 1994), 110.

18 "Never, Never, Never . . .": Daniel Todman, *Britain's War: A New World, 1942– 1947* (Allen Lane, 2020), 692.

18 "We want to employ": James S. Sutterlin, "Interview with Alger Hiss" [1990], *United Nations Oral History Project* 3 <https://digitallibrary.un.org /record/474711?ln=en> accessed 1 November 2021.

18 That man was Ralph Bunche: *Ibid.*, 12.

18 "dictates of humanity": *Application Instituting Proceedings, Corfu Channel Case (UK v Albania)* [1949], International Court of Justice [hereafter ICJ] Application, British Memorial and Annexes, 9.

18 "hardest working conference": Urquhart, *Ralph Bunche*, 117–19.

19 The words were bold: Oeter, "Self-Determination," para 6.

19 "Not as good as I would like": Urquhart, *Ralph Bunche*, 121.

20 A catalyst for change: 2 International Military Tribunal at Nuremberg [hereafter IMT), 32.

20 *Lebensraum* was brutal: *Ibid.*, 57.

20 with the power to prosecute: Agreement for the Prosecution and Punishment of the Major War Criminals of the European Axis, and Establishing the Charter of the International Military Tribunal (8 August 1945), 82 UNTS 279–84 (annex), Article 6(c).

20 The charges against many: 2 IMT, 42.

20 "a right of self-determination": 3 IMT (13th day).

20 "aggressive warfare": 2 IMT, 105.

20 emphasised the legitimacy: 3 IMT (12th day).

20 Germany's war against it: *Ibid.*

21 The 1949 Geneva Convention: Geneva Convention (IV) relative to the Protection of Civilian Persons in Time of War (12 August 1949, into force 21 October 1950), 75 UNTS 287, Article 49(1).

21 Britain actively supported: The United Kingdom signed the Convention on 8 December 1949 and ratified it on 23 September 1957. "Status of Signatures and Ratifications Geneva Convention (IV) Relative to the Protection of Civilian Persons in Time of War" <https://ihl-databases.icrc.org/applic/ihl /ihl.nsf/States.xsp?xp_viewStates=XPages_NORMStatesParties&xp_treaty Selected=380> accessed 1 November 2021.

21 he was a figure of inspiration: Peter Pan, "The Challenge of University Education," *Mauritius Times*, 24 May 1957.

22 One of these protocols: Protocol No. 4 to the Convention for the Protection of Human Rights and Fundamental Freedoms, securing certain rights and freedoms other than those already included in the Convention and in the first Protocol thereto, as amended by Protocol No. 11 (16 September 1963, into force 2 May 1968), 46 ETS 1, Articles 3(1), 4.

22 Britain never signed it: Chart of Signatures and Ratifications of Treaty 046 (ECHR Protocol 4) (*Council of Europe*) <https://www.coe.int/en/web

/conventions/full-list/-/conventions/treaty/046/signatures?p_auth=MZr6n
Tco> accessed 5 November 2019.

23 It was said by some: Nigel Wenban-Smith and Marina Carter, *Chagos: A History* (Chagos Conservation Trust, 2016), 17–18; Nigel Wenban-Smith, *Conceicao History* (2021), note on file with author.

23 "group of black people": Bernardo Gomes de Brito, *História Trágico-Marítima: Em que se escrevem chronologicamente os naufrágios que tiverão as naus de Portugal, depois que se poz em exercício a Navegação de India* (1735) (Classic Reprint), vol. 1 (Forgotten Books, 2018).

23 The enslaved of Peros Banhos: Peter Burroughs, "The Mauritius Rebellion of 1832 and the Abolition of British Colonial Slavery," *Journal of Imperial and Commonwealth History*, 4 (1976), 243–65.

24 It is not easy to glean: "Chagos and Peros Banhos" (*Emily Grace*, 3 June 2012) <http://mvemilygrace.blogspot.com/2012/06/chagos-and-peros-banhos.html> accessed 3 November 2021.

25 "pocket handkerchief paradise": Sumathi Ramaswamy, *The Lost Land of Lemuria* (University of California Press, 2004), 233 (citing Sir Hilary Blood, "The Peaks of Lemuria," *Geographical Magazine*, 29:10 [February 1957], 516–22).

27 "My father just told us": In November 2021, in Crawley, I met with a [cousin] of Liseby's, Joseph [Volly], who shared a little more information about the family ("My grandparents were born on Peros Banhos, on Six Iles, our ancestors came from Mozambique, my great-great-grandfather, I think, a slave, came to work on copra industry. Liseby's father worked as a gardener, he knew all about medicinal plants, and he liked to tell stories").

27 There was a hospital: Fernand Mandarin, "Living Memories: A Worker's View of the 1950s," in Nigel Wenban Smith and Marina Carter, *Chagos: A History* (Chagos Conservation Trust, 2016), 422–44. See also Mary Darlow, "Report by Public Assistance Commissioner and Social Welfare Advisor," Port Louis, *PRO*, CO1023/132 (1953).

28 In the "go-down": Fernand Mandarin, unpublished memoir, recorded by Robert Furlong in Wenban-Smith and Carter, *Chagos*, 419.

PART TWO: 1966

33 he was a man of his times: David Lowe, *Australian Between Empires: The Life of Percy Spender* (Routledge, 2010), 183–84.

33 He vigorously defended: Jean Spender, *Ambassador's Wife* (Angus & Robertson, 1968), 114, 136, 143, 152.

33 He enjoyed life: *Ibid.*, 163, 165.

34 "Negro grooms": *Ibid.*, 155.

34 "We must all accept it": Harold Macmillan, "The Wind of Change Speech" (3 February 1960) <https://web-archives.univ-pau.fr/english/TD2doc1.pdf> accessed 1 November 2021.

34 At the General Assembly: "Reports of the Special Committee on Information Transmitted Under Article 73e of the Charter (1947–1951)" <https://digitallibrary.un.org/search?ln=en&as=1&m1=e&p1=Report+of+the+Special+Committee+on+Information+Transmitted+under+Article+73e+of+the

+Charter&f1=830&op1=a&m2=a&p2=&f2=&op2=a&m3=a&p3=&f3=&rm =&ln=en&action_search=Search&fti=0&sf=year&so=d&rg=25&sc=0&c= United+Nations+Digital+Library+System&of=hb> accessed 3 November 2021; "Reports of the Committee on Information from Non-Self-Governing Territories (1952–1963)" <3 November 2021>; Jessica Lynne Pearson, "Defending Empire at the United Nations: The Politics of International Colonial Oversight in the Era of Decolonisation," *Journal of Imperial and Commonwealth History*, 45 (2017), 525, 531–33.

35 Britain was not planning to leave: Pearson, "Defending Empire at the United Nations," 526, citing Alan Burns, *In Defence of Colonies* (George Allen and Unwin, 1957), 5.

35 "colour prejudice in reverse": *Ibid.*

35 "worldwide contest": Pearson, "Defending Empire at the United Nations," 540–41.

35 Such bases had to remain: "United States Policy Toward Dependent Territories, Paper Prepared by the Colonial Policy Review Sub-Committee of the Committee on Problems of Dependent Areas (26 April 1950) FRUS 1952-54, III UN Affairs 775" (Office of the Historian, US Department of State, 26 April 1950), 1078 <https://history.state.gov/historicaldocuments/frus1952-54v03/d775> accessed 5 November 2019.

35 declared colonialism to be "an evil": "Final Communiqué of the Asian-African Conference of Bandung" (24 April 1955) <https://www.cvce.eu/en/obj/final _communique_of_the_asian_african_conference_of_bandung_24_april _1955-en-676237bd-72f7-471f-949a-88b6ae513585.html> accessed 3 November 2021.

36 President Dwight D. Eisenhower recognised: UNGA [United Nations General Assembly] A_PV-868-EN (15th session, 868th plenary meeting, Thursday, 22 September 1960), 45.

36 a goal of "political independence": UNGA A_PV-877-EN (15th session, 877th plenary meeting, Thursday, 29 September 1960), 225.

36 He expressed the hope: UNGA A_PV-935-EN (15th session, 935th plenary meeting, Monday, 5 December 1960), 1139, paras 112–13 (Mr. Aiken).

36 The US State Department hoped: Ebere Nwaubani, "The United States and the Liquidation of European Colonial Rule in Tropical Africa, 1941–1963," *Cahiers d'études africaines*, XLIII (2003), 505, 528.

37 A chastened delegate: UNGA A_PV-947-EN (15th session, 947th plenary meeting, Wednesday, 14 December 1960), para 48.

37 an act that Germany has recently recognised: Philip Oltermann, "Germany Agrees to Pay Namibia 1.1bn Euros Over Historical Herero-Nama Genocide," *Guardian*, 28 May 2021.

38 requesting an advisory opinion: James Crawford and Paul Mertenskötter, "The South West Africa Cases (1949 to 1971) (Ch. 11)," *Landmark Cases in Public International Law*, Eirik Bjorge and Cameron Miles (eds), (Kindle, Hart, 2017), s. I.

38 In short, the Court ruled: *International Status of South-West Africa (Advisory Opinion)* [1950], ICJ Rep 128, 143–44.

38 the Court gave a second advisory opinion: *South-West Africa—Voting Procedure (Advisory Opinion)* [1955], ICJ Rep 67.

38 a third advisory opinion: *Admissibility of Hearings of Petitioners by the Committee on South West Africa (Advisory Opinion)* [1956], ICJ Rep 23, 32.

38 "a place of progressive potential": Crawford and Mertenskötter, "The South West Africa Cases," sub-s. IV.A.

38 South Africa's persistent disregard: *South-West Africa—Voting Procedure (Advisory Opinion)* (Sep Op J. Lauterpacht) [1955], ICJ Rep 90, 120.

38 The General Assembly picked up: UNGA Res 1142 (XII) (709th plenary meeting, 25 October 1957) (Legal action to ensure the fulfilment of the obligations assumed by the Union of South Africa in respect of the Territory of South West Africa); UNGA Res 1361 (XIV) (838th plenary meeting, 17 November 1959) (Legal action to ensure the fulfilment of the obligations assumed by the Union of South Africa in respect of the Territory of South West Africa).

38 It retained the services of: Michael T. Kaufman, "Ernest Gross, a Key Diplomat During Cold War, Dies at 92," *New York Times*, 4 May 1999 <https://www.nytimes.com/1999/05/04/world/ernest-gross-a-key-diplomat-during-cold-war-dies-at-92.html> accessed 4 November 2021.

39 Ethiopia promptly followed suit: Carol A. Johnson, "Conferences of Independent African States," *International Organization*, 16 (1962), 426, 428–29; see also "Conferences of Independent African States" <https://encyclopedia2.thefreedictionary.com/Conferences+of+Independent+African+States> accessed 4 November 2021.

39 Liberia and Ethiopia filed: *South West Africa Cases (Ethiopia v South Africa; Liberia v South Africa) (Preliminary Objections)* [1962], ICJ Rep 319, 322–26.

39 they wanted to end apartheid: *Pleadings (Application) South West Africa Cases (Ethiopia v South Africa; Liberia v South Africa)* [1966], ICJ Pleadings 1, para 4.

39 which South Africa argued: *Pleadings (Respondent's Memorial of Preliminary Objections) South West Africa Cases (Ethiopia v South Africa; Liberia v South Africa) (Preliminary Objections)* [1961], ICJ Pleadings 212 376 et seq.

39 By a narrow majority: *South West Africa Cases (Ethiopia v South Africa; Liberia v South Africa) (Preliminary Objections)*, 342–44, 347.

39 The two jointly wrote: *South West Africa Cases (Ethiopia v South Africa; Liberia v South Africa) (Preliminary Objections) (Joint Diss Op J Spender & J Fitzmaurice)* [1966], ICJ Rep 465.

39 "well-being and the social progress": *Ibid.*, 466–67.

39 with the active assistance: Lowe, *Australian Between Empires*, 167.

40 one died, another fell ill: Judge Abdel Hamid Badawi (Egypt) died in August 1965; Judge José Bustamante y Rivero (Peru) was ill.

40 "Head and shoulders above": Victor Kattan, "Decolonizing the International Court of Justice: The Experience of Judge Sir Muhammad Zafrulla Khan in the South West Africa Cases," *Asian Journal of International Law*, 5 (2015), 310, 317, fn 34 (citing "The Election of Judges to the International Court of Justice" [very confidential] by W.E. Beckett, 19 January 1946, DO 35/1216. TNA).

40 "fanatical anti-colonial": "Letter to the United Nations Political Department, Foreign Office, from the United Kingdom Delegation to the United Nations, FO 371/112421/255/124 (9 October 1954)."

40 In 1960 he declined: *South West Africa Cases (Ethiopia v South Africa; Liberia v South Africa) (Correspondence)* [1960], ICJ Rep 510, 534.

40 was not entirely welcome to Spender: Lowe, *Australian Between Empires*, 175.

40 "substantial majority": *Ibid.*, 156.

40 "We will be appreciative": *Ibid.*, 166, 192.

41 "extremely difficult to influence": Kattan, "Decolonizing the International Court of Justice," 316, fns 27, 29 (citing a confidential telegram sent from the Foreign Office in London to the United Kingdom Delegation to the UN, 19 November 1954, signed by Kelvin White on behalf of P.E. Ramsbotham in "Election of the Successor to the Late Sir Benegal Rau as Judge at the ICJ," 14 December 1954, DO 35/7123 TNA).

41 "old friend": Spender, *Ambassador's Wife*, 113.

41 As Spender articulated: Lowe, *Australian Between Empires*, 168 (citing Peter Garran, The Hague, letter to Sir Roger Alan, 21 July 1966, FO371/188151 TNA).

41 the Court reversed that ruling: *Barcelona Traction, Light and Power Company, Limited (Belgium v Spain)* [1970], ICJ Rep, 3 paras 33–36; *Application of the Convention on the Prevention and Punishment of the Crime of Genocide (The Gambia v Myanmar) (23 January 2020) (Prov Measures)* [2020], ICJ Gen List 178 1, para 41.

42 "completely unfounded": *South West Africa Cases, Second Phase (Diss Op J Jessup)* [1966], ICJ Rep 325.

42 "the intelligence of a future day": *Ibid.*

42 who reprimanded him: *South West Africa Cases, Second Phase (Declaration J Spender)* [1966], ICJ Rep 51, para 28.

42 Some saw the decision: James Crawford, "'Dreamers of the Day': Australia and the International Court of Justice," *Melbourne Journal of International Law*, 14 (2013), 520, 536.

42 "There were no grounds": "I never disqualified myself. There were no grounds for disqualifying me. The President of the Court (Sir Percy Spender) was of the view that it would be improper for me to sit, as I had at one time been nominated judge ad hoc for the applicant States (Liberia and Ethiopia), though I had not sat in that capacity. I disagreed entirely with that view and gave the President my reasons, which I still consider were good reasons. But he told me that a large majority of the judges agreed with him that I should not sit. So I had no option." *Observer* (London, 31 July 1966), 22.

42 Many . . . considered the Court: Ernest A. Gross, "The South West Africa Case: What Happened?" [1966], *Foreign Affairs* <https://www.foreignaffairs.com/articles/namibia/1966-10-01/south-west-africa-case-what-happened> accessed 5 November 2019.

43 One hundred and fourteen countries voted: UNGA Res 2145 (XXI) (1454th plenary meeting, 27 October 1966) (Question of South West Africa).

43 The Assembly changed: UNGA Res 2372 (XXII) (1671th plenary meeting, 12 June 1968) (Question of South West Africa).

43 "All peoples have the right": International Covenant on Civil and Political Rights (adopted 16 December 1966, into force 23 March 1976), 999 UNTS 14668, Article 1.

43 Spender retired: Crawford and Mertenskötter, "The South West Africa Cases," s. V.

44 "certain small British-owned": David Vine, *Island of Shame: The Secret History of the U.S. Military Base on Diego Garcia* (Princeton University Press, 2009), 71–76.

44 "Strategic Island Concept": *Ibid.*, 56–63. Barber's son wrote: "[My father] was not aware [. . .] of what was happening to the islanders. In fact he was among those being fed the fictions that there was no population in Diego Garcia beyond a small number of transient plantation contract laborers [. . .] He was shocked at the callousness and cruelty of how these evacuations were conducted. Now with the damage done, he believed it was imperative for the US and British governments to make substantial reparations": Richard Barber, "'Island of Shame': An Exchange on Diego Garcia," *New York Review of Books* (2009) <https://www.nybooks.com/articles/2009/07/02/island-of-shame-an-exchange-on-diego-garcia/> accessed 10 November 2021.

45 "We have the power": UK Foreign Office, Colonial Office and Ministry of Defence, "US Defence Interests in the Indian Ocean, D.O. (O)(64)23, FCO 31/3437 (23 April 1964)," paras 8 and 11.

45 "confront the Mauritians": *Ibid.*, paras 11–12.

46 The British recognised Chagos: Robert Newton, "Report on the Anglo-American Survey in the Indian Ocean," CO 1036/1332 (1964), paras 48, 49, 60, 67.

46 "as rapidly as possible": Jonathan Coleman, "Harold Wilson, Lyndon Johnson and the Vietnam War, 1964–68" (American Studies Today Online, 7 December 2004) <http://www.americansc.org.uk/online/Wilsonjohnson.htm> accessed 10 November 2021.

46 "Generous compensation": "Telegram from the Foreign Office to Washington, No 3582, FO 371/184523" (30 April 1965), para 3.

47 "The Prime Minister may therefore wish": "UK Colonial Office, 'Note for the Prime Minister's Meeting with Sir Seewoosagur Ramgoolam, Premier of Mauritius' PREM 13/3320" (22 September 1965), 1, 5.

47 "Not acceptable": "United Kingdom, 'Record of a Meeting Held in Lancaster House at 2:30 p.m. on Thursday 23rd September: Mauritius Defence Matters,' CO 1036/1253" (23 September 1965), para 3.

47 The British agreed: *Ibid.*, para 22.

48 the British and the Americans were informed: "United Kingdom, 'Record of UK–US Talks on Defence Facilities in the Indian Ocean,' FO 371/184529 (23–24 September 1965)" (23 September 1965); "Summary Record of 'Plenary' Meeting between the United Kingdom and United States Officials (Led by Mr. Kitchen), Mr. Peck in the Chair on 24 September 1965."

48 Britain announced the decision: "UK Colonial Office, 'Mauritius Constitutional Conference Report' (24 September 1965)," para 20.

48 "as soon as possible": "UK Foreign Office, 'Minute from Secretary of State for the Colonies to the Prime Minister,' FO 371/184529 (5 November 1965)," paras 5–6.

48 "lay ourselves open": *Ibid.*, paras 6–9.

48 "concert tactics": "Telegram from the UK Foreign Office to the UK Mission to the UN, No 4310, FO 371/184529 (6 November 1965)," para 5; "Telegram from the UK Foreign Office to the UK Mission to the UN, No 4327 (8 November 1965)," para 2(h).

48 "no permanent inhabitants": "Telegram from the UK Mission to the UN to the UK Foreign Office, No 2837 (8 November 1965)," para 4.

49 "We detach these islands": *Chagos Islanders v Attorney General & HM BIOT Commissioner* [2003], EWHC 222 (QB) [70] (Ouseley J).

49 "nothing wrong in law": UK Foreign Office, "Minute Written by Anthony Aust, FO Legal Adviser (23 Oct 1968)"; UK Foreign Office, "Minute 'Immigration Legislation for BIOT' (Anthony Aust, FO Legal Adviser) (16 Jan 1970)."

49 The General Assembly quickly passed: UNGA Res 2066 (XX) (1398th plenary meeting, 16 December 1965) (Question of Mauritius).

50 A second resolution followed: UNGA Res 2232 (XXI) (1500th plenary meeting, 20 December 1966) (Question of American Samoa, Antigua, Bahamas, Bermuda, British Virgin Islands, Grenada, Guam, Mauritius, Montserrat, New Hebrides, Niue, Pitcairn, St. Helena, St. Kitts-Nevis-Anguilla, St. Lucia, St. Vincent, Seychelles, Solomon Islands, Tokelau Islands, Turks and Caicos Islands, and the United States Virgin Islands).

50 That too was ignored: UNGA Res 2357 (XXII) (1641th plenary meeting, 19 December 1967) (Question of American Samoa, Antigua, Bahamas, Bermuda, British Virgin Islands, Grenada, Guam, Mauritius, Montserrat, New Hebrides, Niue, Pitcairn, St. Helena, St. Kitts-Nevis-Anguilla, St. Lucia, St. Vincent, Seychelles, Solomon Islands, Tokelau Islands, Turks and Caicos Islands, and the United States Virgin Islands).

51 "sacred trust": Charter of the United Nations (26 June 1945, into force 24 October 1945), 59 Stat 1031, Article 73 (Chapter XI).

51 "very tough": "Diplomatic Cable Signed by D.A. Greenhill (24 Aug 1966)" <https://commons.wikimedia.org/wiki/File:Diplomatic_Cable_signed_by _D.A._Greenhill,_dated_August_24,_1966.jpg> accessed 12 November 2021.

52 "Along with the Birds": "Diplomatic Cable Signed by D.A. Greenhill (24 Aug 1966)."

52 following a decision: David Snoxell, "Denis Healey and the Chagos Archipelago," *Guardian*, 8 October 2015 (letter); David Snoxell, "Anglo/American Complicity in the Removal of the Inhabitants of the Chagos Islands, 1964–73," *Journal of Imperial and Colonial History*, 37 (2009), 127–34.

52 Years later, some who were deported: Laura Jeffery, *Chagos Islanders in Mauritius and the UK: Forced Displacement and Onward Migration* (Manchester University Press, 2011), 95–108.

52 "required only Diego Garcia"; "They had no objections": M.W. Hewitt, EAD, to W.A. Ward, High Commissioner Mauritius, 4 December 1980, FO 119 of FCO file 31/2770.

52 about 1,500 people: Richard Gifford and Richard Dunne, "A Dispossessed People: The Depopulation of the Chagos Archipelago 1965–1973," *Population Space and Place*, 20 (2014), 37–49.

52 When this solution failed: Vine, *Island of Shame*, 113–14.

53 "wizened, bony": Geoffrey Trease, *This Is Your Century* (Heinemann, 1965), 300.

53 "The child usually gets its way": *Ibid.*, 306.

53 John Rawling Todd: "British Indian Ocean Territory (Chronology)" <https://www.worldstatesmen.org/Br_Indian_Ocean_Terr.html> accessed 12 November 2021.

55 the MS *Nordvaer*: "Stamps of the British Indian Ocean Territory" (5 December 2008) <https://shipstamps.co.uk/forum/viewtopic.php?t=6422> accessed 12 November 2021.

55 "No one from the government of Mauritius": Conversation with Joseph Bertrand, 24 November 2021.

PART THREE: 1984

60 Clyde Ferguson: "UNESCO Statement on Race and Racial Prejudice," *Current Anthropology*, 9 (1968), 270.
60 "Nicaragua Takes Case": Stuart Taylor Jr., "Nicaragua Takes Case Against U.S. to World Court," *New York Times* (10 April 1984) <https://www.nytimes .com/1984/04/10/world/nicaragua-takes-case-against-us-to-world-court .html?searchResultPosition=9> accessed 10 November 2021.
61 "not in the scope": Mary Thornton, "In the World Court," *Washington Post* (7 December 1984) <https://www.washingtonpost.com/archive/politics/1984 /12/07/in-the-world-court/f9398029-8e4b-47b2-bf80-d82d2572fe19/> accessed 12 November 2021.
61 The two established their own firm: *Ibid.*
61 the speech Mauritian Prime Minister Aneerood Jugnauth gave: "At this juncture I should like to dwell on an issue which affects the vital interests of Mauritius; I mean the Mauritian claim of sovereignty over the Chagos Archipelago, which was excised by the then colonial Power from the territory of Mauritius in contravention of General Assembly resolutions 1514 (XV) and 2066 (XX). This dismemberment of Mauritian territory, the violation of our territorial integrity, has been made all the more unacceptable by the fact that one of the islands of that very Archipelago, Diego García, is now a full-fledged nuclear base, which poses a constant threat to the security of Mauritius and to that of all the littoral and hinterland States of the Indian Ocean, the very Ocean declared to be a zone of peace by this Assembly in 1971." "Verbatim Record of the 34th Meeting, 37th Session, General Assembly, Friday, 15 October 1982," 641, para 68 <https://digitallibrary.un.org/record/36935/files/A_37 PV.34-EN .pdf> accessed 12 November 2021 (Jugnauth).
62 "Absolutely must go": Vine, *Island of Shame*, 111 (citing memorandum for the Deputy Chief of Naval Operations [Plans and Policy], 24 March 1971).
63 The *Washington Post* ran a story: David Ottaway, "Islanders Were Evicted for U.S. Base," *Washington Post*, 9 September 1975; see also "Diego Garcia: The Islanders That Britain Sold," *Sunday Times*, 21 September 1975.
63 Nor did a report: John Madeley, *Diego Garcia: A Contrast to the Falklands*, Minority Rights Group, Report No. 54, August 1982, revised February 1985.
63 The Security Council had ordered: UNSC Res 264 (1969), para 3; UNSC Res 269 (1969), para 5.
63 The Security Council instructed: UNSC Res 264 (1969), para 7; UNSC Res 269 (1969), para 7.
64 The composition of the Court: *Legal Consequences for States of the Continued Presence of South Africa in Namibia (South West Africa) Notwithstanding Security Council Resolution 276 (1970) (Advisory Opinion)* [1971], ICJ Rep 16, 16.
64 The Court's decision: *Ibid.*, para 105.
64 Another resolution, 2145: *Ibid.*, para 106.
64 By a large majority: *Ibid.*, paras 131, 133.

64 "a denial of self-determination": *Legal Consequences for States of the Continued Presence of South Africa in Namibia (South West Africa) Notwithstanding Security Council Resolution 276 (1970) (Advisory Opinion) (Declaration J Khan)* [1971], ICJ Rep 59, 63.

64 Fitzmaurice's lengthy, irritated dissent: *Legal Consequences for States of the Continued Presence of South Africa in Namibia (South West Africa) Notwithstanding Security Council Resolution 276 (1970) (Advisory Opinion) (Diss Op J Fitzmaurice)* [1971], ICJ Rep 208, 220–24, 308.

64 "humanitarian sentiments": *Ibid.*, paras 91, 105.

65 "natural perversity": *Tyrer v UK (Sep Op J Fitzmaurice)* App No 5856/72 (ECtHR, 25 April 1978), para 12.

66 The new rules came with: Tulio Treves, "The United Nations Convention on the Law of the Sea" (UN Audiovisual Library of International Law) <https://legal.un.org/avl/ha/uncls/uncls.html> accessed 12 November 2021.

66 "interests of colonialism": "Third U.N. Conference on the Law of the Sea (A/CONF.62/SR.60) (60th Plenary Meeting, 6 Apr 1976)," 24, para 26 (LAI Ya-Lo, China).

66 Invoking resolution 1514: U.N. Convention on the Law of the Sea (16 November 1994), 1833, UNTS 3, Articles 305–07.

66 Cuba made clear: "Third U.N. Conference on the Law of the Sea (A/CONF.62/SR.61) (61st Plenary Meeting, 6 Apr 1976)," 35, para 55 (D'Stefano Pissani, Cuba); "Third United Nations Conference on the Law of the Sea (A/CONF.62/SR.62) (62nd Plenary Meeting, 7 Apr 1976)," 38–39, para 36 (Ballah, Trinidad & Tobago).

66 Madagascar wanted a new court: "Third U.N. Conference on the Law of the Sea (A/CONF.62/SR.61) (61st Plenary Meeting, 6 Apr 1976)," (n. 139) 34, para 44 (Ranjeva, Madagascar).

66 as did Nigeria: *Ibid.*, 35, para 59 (Adeniji, Nigeria).

66 Mauritius proposed arbitration: "Third U.N. Conference on the Law of the Sea (A/CONF.62/SR.62) (62nd Plenary Meeting, 7 Apr 1976)," (n. 139) 37, para 12 (Gayan, Mauritius).

66 "the aspirations": *Ibid.*, 39, para 46 (Locato, Ecuador).

66 "a larger role": "Third U.N. Conference on the Law of the Sea (A/CONF.62/SR.63) (63rd Plenary Meeting, 8 Apr 1976)," 44, para 3 (Akrum, Surinam).

66 Bangladesh and Indonesia: "Third U.N. Conference on the Law of the Sea (A/CONF.62/SR.62) (62nd Plenary Meeting, 7 Apr 1976)," (n. 139) 41, para 65 (Rashid, Bangladesh), 72 (Jusuf, Indonesia).

66 as did Syria: "Third U.N. Conference on the Law of the Sea (A/CONF.62/SR.63) (63rd Plenary Meeting, 8 Apr 1976)," (n. 144) 45, para 14 (Sibahi, Syria).

66 and the United Arab Emirates: "Third U.N. Conference on the Law of the Sea (A/CONF.62/SR.64) (64th Plenary Meeting, 9 Apr 1976)," 49, para 28 (Al-Mour, UAE).

66 Ireland expressed doubts: *Ibid.*, 47, para 9 (Costello, Ireland).

67 the Somozas were toppled: *Military and Paramilitary Activities in and against Nicaragua (Nicaragua v US) (Merits)* [1986], ICJ Rep 14, paras 18–25.

67 President Reagan imposed: *Ibid.*, paras 75–125.

67 the main aim was to shift: Paul S. Reichler, "Holding America to Its Own Best

Standards: Abe Chayes and Nicaragua in the World Court," *Harvard International Law Journal*, 42 (2001), 15, 22.

68 "as a law-abiding nation": *Ibid.*, 23.

68 Many thought Nicaragua had a strong case: *Ibid.*, 24.

68 "unequivocal": Reichler, "Holding America."

68 Nicaragua filed a case: Robert Kolb, "Military and Paramilitary Activities in and against Nicaragua (Nicaragua v. United States) (1984 to 1986) (Ch. 15)," Eirik Bjorge and Cameron Miles (eds), *Landmark Cases in Public International Law* (Kindle, Hart, 2017), s. II.

68 the Court ordered provisional measures: *Military and Paramilitary Activities in and against Nicaragua (Nicaragua v US) (Provisional Measures)* [1984], ICJ Rep 169; Augusto Zamora, "La Haya: Un Juicio para La Historia" [1991], *Envío* <https://www.envio.org.ni/articulo/682> accessed 12 November 2021.

69 The US reaction: *Military and Paramilitary Activities in and against Nicaragua (Nicaragua v US) (Merits)* [1986], ICJ Rep 14, para 10.

69 The State Department asserted: Bernard Weinraub, "U.S. Limits Its Role at Court in Hague," *New York Times* (8 October 1985), 5.

69 argued for an expansive interpretation: W. Michael Reisman, "Coercion and Self-Determination: Construing Article 2(4)," *American Journal of International Law*, 78 (1984), 642.

69 "popular will": *Ibid.*, 644.

69 "enhance": *Ibid.*, 643–44.

69 "rape common sense": *Ibid.*, 645.

70 They rejected the US argument: *Military and Paramilitary Activities in and against Nicaragua (Nicaragua v US) (Merits)* [1986], ICJ Rep 14, para 292. In September 1991, following Nicaragua's decision to discontinue the proceedings, the case is concluded. *Military and Paramilitary Activities in and against Nicaragua (Nicaragua v United States) (Discontinuance/Removal from List)* [1991], ICJ Rep 47.

70 "in pursuance of": *Ibid.*

70 "What is a colony": *Military and Paramilitary Activities in and against Nicaragua (Nicaragua v US) (Merits) (Diss Op J Schwebel)* [1986], ICJ Rep 259, para 180.

71 "loss of sovereignty": "U.K. House of Commons, Written Answers: Foreign and Commonwealth Affairs—Indian Ocean, FCO 31/3836 (21 Oct. 1975)," 130; "United Kingdom, Anglo/US Consultations on the Indian Ocean: November 1975-Agenda Item III, Brief No. 4: Future of Aldabra, Farquar and Desroches, FCO 40/687 (Nov 1975)," para 2(a).

71 a further £650,000: Mauritius letter from Prime Minister Sir S. Ramgoolam to British High Commission, Port Louis, 4 September 1972.

72 To obtain a payment: Agreement concerning the Ilois from the Chagos Archipelago (7 July 1982, into force 28 October 1982), 1316 UNTS 21924.

73 a UN human rights body: Commission on Human Rights, Sub-Commission on the Promotion and Protection of Human Rights, Working Group on Minorities, Report on the Visit by the Working Group to Mauritius, Examining Possible Solutions to Problems Involving Minorities, Including the Promotion of Mutual Understanding Between and Among Minorities and Governments, U.N. Doc. E/CN.4/Sub.2/AC.5/2002/2 (3 April 2002), para 37.

73 To justify their actions: Denzil Dunnett, "Self-Determination and the Falk-lands," *International Affairs* (Royal Institute of International Affairs), 59 (1983), 415–16.

73 the British government would even publish a paper: "2010 to 2015 Govern-ment Policy: Falkland Islanders' Right to Self-Determination (Policy Paper) (Updated 8 May 2015)" <https://www.gov.uk/government/publications/2010 -to-2015-government-policy-falkland-islanders-right-to-self-deter mination/2010-to-2015-government-policy-falkland-islanders-right-to-self -determination> accessed 14 November 2021.

73 Olivier Bancoult . . . embarked on: Olivier Bancoult, "The Historic Legal Battle of the Chagossians to Return to Their Homeland, the Chagos Islands, and to Be Compensated for Their Deportation: A Narrative," *South Africa Yearbook of International Law*, 29 (2014), 21.

74 The power to legislate: *R (on the application of Bancoult) v Secretary of State for the Foreign and Commonwealth Office* [2001], Q.B. 1067, para 5.

75 "shameful" . . . "pauperisation and expulsion": *Chagos Islanders v Attorney General & HM British Indian Ocean Commissioner* [2004], EWCA Civ 997.

76 "irrational" . . . "[T]he right of abode": *R (On the Application of Bancoult No 2) v Secretary of State for Foreign and Commonwealth Affairs* [2008], UKHL 61, paras 45, 49 (Lord Hoffmann).

76 "the law gives it" . . . "entitled, on the advice of": *R v Secretary of State,* UKHL 61, paras 45, 49 (Lord Hoffmann).

76 Lord Bingham wrote a strong dissent: *Ibid.*, para 72 (Lord Bingham).

76 on the grounds that: *Chagos Islanders v UK (admissibility)*, App No. 35622/04 (ECtHR, 11 December 2012), paras 77–83.

76 "non justiciable political": *Olivier Bancoult et al v Robert McNamara et al*, US Court of Appeals, D.C. Circuit, 21 April 2006.

77 "inalienable right to human dignity": "Nelson Mandela's Inaugural Speech (Pretoria, 11 May 1994)" <https://www.africa.upenn.edu/Articles_Gen/Inau gural_Speech_17984.html> accessed 13 November 2021.

77 In time, the parties to the Convention: "Decision of Conference of the Parties to the Convention on Biological Diversity (UNEP/CBD/COP/DEC/VII/5) (13 Apr 2004) (Marine and Coastal Diversity)," paras 10–31 <https://www.cbd .int/doc/decisions/cop-07/cop-07-dec-05-en.pdf> accessed 12 November 2021.

77 The Security Council created . . . in the former Yugoslavia: UNSC Res 827 (1993).

77 and Rwanda: UNSC Res 955 (1994).

78 Yet the Court also recognised: *Legality of the Threat or Use of Nuclear Weapons* (Advisory Opinion) [1996], ICJ Rep 226, para 29; *Pleadings Legality of the Threat or Use of Nuclear Weapons (written submissions of the United Kingdom)* [1995], ICJ Pleadings 1, 61–64.

78 as counsel for Samoa: *Pleadings Legality of the Threat or Use of Nuclear Weapons (Verbatim Record 3 Nov 1995, CR 95/31) (Samoa's Submissions)* [1995], ICJ Plead-ings 1, 36.

78 Spain retained a couple of enclaves: Ceuta and Melilla.

78 two islands were under French rule: Réunion and Mayotte.

78 "In 2001 I had a fifteen-day demonstration": "Interview of David Raymond

Snoxell by Malcolm McBain" (19 November 2007), 38 <https://www.chu.cam
.ac.uk/media/uploads/files/Snoxell.pdf> accessed 13 November 2021.

79   "ventriloquised": *Ibid.*, 40.

79   The US response: Philippe Sands, *Torture Team* (Weidenfeld & Nicolson,
2008).

79   "Contrary to earlier": Mark Tran, "Miliband Admits US Rendition Flights
Stopped on UK Soil," *Guardian* (21 February 2008) <https://www.theguardian
.com/world/2008/feb/21/ciarendition.usa> accessed 12 November 2021.

80   In 2015 a senior State Department official: Ian Cobain, "CIA Interrogated Suspects on Diego Garcia, Says Colin Powell Aide," *Guardian* (30 January 2015)
<https://www.theguardian.com/world/2015/jan/30/cia-interrogation-diego
-garcia-lawrence-wilkerson> accessed 12 November 2021.

80   This was unclear: Matt Dathan, "Diego Garcia Rendition Flight Logs
'Destroyed'," *The Times* (10 July 2014) <https://www.thetimes.co.uk/article/diego
-garcia-rendition-flight-logs-destroyed-7pqonosmcjo> accessed 6 May 2022.

80   deplored the failure of British oversight: UK House of Commons Foreign
Affairs Committee, "Seventh Report of Session 2007–08 (Overseas Territories)
(HC 147-I)" (18 June 2008), para 4 <https://publications.parliament.uk/pa
/cm200708/cmselect/cmfaff/147/147i.pdf> accessed 12 November 2021.

80   The US Senate Select Committee: "The Use of Diego Garcia for Rendition (Foreign Affairs Committee)" (UK Parliament, 19 June 2014), para 15
<https://publications.parliament.uk/pa/cm201415/cmselect/cmfaff/377/37704
.htm#n15> accessed 12 November 2021.

80   Coincidentally, it was during this time: Laura Jeffrey, "How a Plantation
Became Paradise: Changing Representations of the Homeland Among Displaced Chagossian Islanders," 13 *Journal of the Royal Anthropological Institute*
951, at 969 (2007).

80   He prepared a lengthy memorandum: Ian Brownlie, "Certain Questions
Relating to the Status of the Chagos Archipelago: Together with Advice on
Options Available to the Government of Mauritius (Opinion, 15 Dec 2003),"
69 (on file with author).

80   Around this time, the Court gave an advisory: *Legal Consequences of the Construction of a Wall in the Occupied Palestinian Territory (Advisory Opinion)*
[2004], ICJ Rep 136, paras 88, 123.

80   Britain's acceptance of the Court's jurisdiction: "House of Commons—
Written Ministerial Statements [6 July 2004] Parliamentary Under-Secretary
of State for Foreign and Commonwealth Affairs (Mr. Bill Rammell),
Column 33WS" <https://publications.parliament.uk/pa/cm200304/cmhansrd
/vo040706/wmstext/40706mo2.htm> accessed 12 November 2021; "Declaration of the UK Accepting the Jurisdiction of the ICJ as Compulsory (Art 36(2)
ICJ Statute)" (22 February 2017) <https://www.icj-cij.org/en/declarations/gb>
accessed 12 November 2021.

81   "Mauritius envisages": *Weekend* (27 June 2004); *Le Mauricien* (28 June 2004).

81   prompting the Foreign Office to amend: "Declaration of the UK Accepting
the Jurisdiction of the ICJ as Compulsory (Art 36(2) ICJ Statute)" (22 February 2017) <https://www.icj-cij.org/en/declarations/gb> accessed 12 November
2021, para 1(ii).

81 "The Government have acted": "House of Commons—Written Ministerial Statements [6 July 2004] Parliamentary Under-Secretary of State for
Foreign and Commonwealth Affairs (Mr. Bill Rammell), Column 33WS"
<https://publications.parliament.uk/pa/cm200304/cmhansrd/vo040706
/wmstext/40706mo2.htm> accessed 12 November 2021.

PART FOUR: 2003

85 Many of the planes: Rebecca Grant, "Iraqi Freedom and the Air Force," *Air
Force Magazine*, March 2013, 38.

85 Jagdish Koonjul . . . told the Council: "Security Council Holds First Debate
on Iraq Since Start of Military Action; Speakers Call for Halt to Aggression,
Immediate Withdrawal (Press Release, SC/7705)" (26 March 2003) <https://
www.un.org/press/en/2003/sc7705.doc.htm> accessed 14 November 2021.

85 *The Times* of London ran a piece: Christopher Greenwood QC, "Britain's War
on Saddam Had the Law on Its Side," *The Times* (22 October 2003); also available in *Yearbook of Islamic & Middle Eastern Law Online*, vol. 9, 29.

86 The "safest legal course": Philippe Sands, *Lawless World: America and the Making and Breaking of Global Rules* (Penguin, 2006), 264.

86 "the Solicitor General, two officials": *Ibid.*, 260.

87 and the authorisation that followed: UK House of Commons Foreign Affairs
Committee, "Seventh Report of Session 2007–08 (Overseas Territories) (HC
147-I)" (18 June 2008), 346; "The Use of Diego Garcia for Rendition (Foreign Affairs Committee)" (UK Parliament, 19 June 2014), para 15 <https://
publications.parliament.uk/pa/cm201415/cmselect/cmfaff/377/37704
.htm#n15> accessed 12 November 2021.

90 A Working Group on Minorities raised concerns: Commission on Human
Rights, Sub-Commission on the Promotion and Protection of Human Rights,
Working Group on Minorities, Report on the Visit by the Working Group
to Mauritius, Examining Possible Solutions to Problems Involving Minorities, Including the Promotion of Mutual Understanding Between and Among
Minorities and Governments, U.N. Doc. E/CN.4/Sub.2/AC.5/2002/2 (3 April
2002), paras 45–55.

90 The Human Rights Committee recommended: Consideration of Reports submitted by the UK under Article 40 of the Covenant (CCPR/C/GBR/CO/6)
(30 July 2008), para 22.

90 The Committee on the Elimination of Racial Discrimination recommended:
Committee on the Elimination of Racial Discrimination, Concluding Obser-
vations, CERD/C/GBR/CO/18-20 (14 September 2011), para 12.

90 "the power to change the fate": G. Le Clézio, "Lavez l'injustice faite aux
Chagossiens," *Le Monde* (17 October 2009) <https://www.lemonde.fr/idees
/article/2009/10/17/lavez-l-injustice-faite-aux-chagossiens-par-jean-marie-g
-le-clezio_1255254_3232.html> accessed 14 November 2021.

91 Mr. Miliband announced that: Paul Rincon, "UK Sets Up Chagos Islands
Marine Reserve," *BBC News* (1 April 2010) <http://news.bbc.co.uk/2/mobile
/science/nature/8599125.stm> accessed 15 November 2021.

91 A "historic victory": "One Year On: The World's Largest Marine Reserve"

(Chagos Conservation Trust, 10 June 2010) <https://chagos-trust.org/news
/one-year-on-the-worlds-largest-marine-reserve> accessed 16 November 2021.

94 Of particular interest was a 2009 cable: "HMG Floats Proposal for Marine
Reserve Covering the Chagos Archipelago (British Indian Ocean Territory)
(15 May 2009)" (WikiLeaks) <https://wikileaks.org/plusd/cables/09LONDON
1156_a.html> accessed 17 November 2019.

94 The proposal would create no difficulties: "HMG Floats Proposal for Marine
Reserve," U.S. cable dated 15 May 2009, para 7, available at https://www
.theguardian.com/world/us-embassy-cables-documents/207149. Under cross-
examination in later litigation, Mr. Roberts accepted that it was likely he
would have said words to the effect that there should be no human footprint
in the Chagos Archipelago other than Diego Garcia, but he denied using the
term "Man Fridays" in relation to the Chagossians: *R (on the application of
Bancoult) v Secretary of State for Foreign and Commonwealth Affairs* [2013],
EWHC 1502 (Admin) (11 June 2013), para 59.

94 The document suggested: *Ibid.*, para 7.

94 the litigation threw up a raft: *R (on the Application of Bancoult No 3) v Secretary
of State for Foreign and Commonwealth Affairs* [2018], UKSC 3.

95 "gravely displeased": Email from counsel in proceedings, 2 February 2021 (on
file with author).

95 The accountancy firm KPMG examined: KPMG, "Feasibility Study for
the Resettlement of the British Indian Ocean Territory" (31 January 2015),
84 et seq <https://www.gov.uk/government/speeches/policy-review-of-resettle
ment-of-the-british-indian-ocean-territory> accessed 16 November 2021.

95 "feasibility, defence and security": "HC Deb 17 Nov 2016, Vol 617 (Hansard)"
<https://hansard.parliament.uk/commons/2016-11-17/debates/DF14B27E
-3DEF-4D46-917D-33E93DDD0C5C/ChagosIslands> accessed 16 November
2021.

95 Bancoult No. 5 is pending on appeal: *R (on the application of Hoareau and Bancoult No 5) v Secretary of State for Foreign and Commonwealth Affairs* [2020],
EWCA Civ 1010; see also Chris Monaghan, "Challenging the United Kingdom's Decision Not to Support the Resettlement of the Chagos Islands: *R (on
the application of Hoareau and Bancoult No 5) v Secretary of State for Foreign and
Commonwealth Affairs* [2020], EWCA Civ 1010 (2021), 26, Judicial Rev 62.

95 "There is no mechanism": Kate McQue, "£40m for Islanders Exiled from
British Territory Goes Unspent," *Guardian* (3 May 2020) <https://www
.theguardian.com/world/2020/may/03/40m-for-islanders-exiled-from-british
-territory-goes-unspent> accessed 16 November 2021.

96 At an earlier stage: *Application of the International Convention on the Elimination of All Forms of Racial Discrimination (Georgia v Russia) (Provisional Measures)* [2011], ICJ Rep 353.

96 the majority found that Georgia had failed: *Application of the International
Convention on the Elimination of All Forms of Racial Discrimination (Georgia v
Russia) (Preliminary Objections)* [2011], ICJ Rep 70, paras 148–84.

97 Judge Greenwood joined the majority: *Ibid.*, 323.

97 The dissenting judges complained: *Ibid., Joint Diss Op J Owada, Simma, Abra-
ham & Donoghue, & J Ad Hoc Gaja* [2011], ICJ Rep 142, para 12.

98 He cited an opinion submitted by Tom Mensah: *Chagos Marine Protected Area Arbitration (Mauritius v UK) (reasoned decision on challenge of arbitrator Greenwood)* [2011], PCA 1, para 77 (citing statement submitted by Judge Mensah).

99 It relied on opinions from: *Ibid.*, paras 91, 164 (citing statements submitted by Judges Higgins and Guillaume).

99 "Why should this tribunal be content": *Pleadings Chagos MPA Arbitration (Mauritius v UK) (Transcript Hearing 4 October 2011 on challenge to J Greenwood).*

99 The four arbitrators came down in favour: *Chagos Marine Protected Area Arbitration (Mauritius v UK) (reasoned decision on challenge of arbitrator Greenwood)*, paras 166–83.

100 "We have no doubts": *Pleadings Chagos MPA Arbitration (Mauritius v UK) (Transcript Hearing day 2 on Jurisdiction & Merits)* [2014] 2 PCA 71, 40.

101 "As a diver myself": *Ibid.*, 48.

101 She ignored the instruction: *Ibid. (Transcript Hearing day 11 on Jurisdiction & Merits)* [2014], 11 PCA 1233, 1318.

101 which was given the herculean task: *Ibid. (Transcript Hearing day 8 on Jurisdiction & Merits)* [2014], 8 PCA 910, 929.

101 Judge Greenwood homed in surgically: *Ibid.*, 980–85.

104 there were "disturbing similarities": *Chagos Marine Protected Area Arbitration (Mauritius v UK) (Dissenting and Concurring Opinion of Judges Kateka and Wolfrum)*, para 91.

105 In 1997, in the *Gabčíkovo-Nagymaros* case: *Gabčíkovo-Nagymaros Project (Hungary/Slovakia)* [1997], ICJ Rep 7, paras 136–47.

106 In 2010, in the *Pulp Mills* case: The Court deferred environmental impact issues to the "Cumulative Impact Study prepared in September 2006 at the request of the International Finance Corporation." *Case Concerning Pulp Mills on the River Uruguay (Argentina v Uruguay)* [2010], ICJ Rep 14, paras 210–14.

106 a fine cross-examination by the Solicitor-General: *Pleadings (hearing CR 2013/14) Whaling in the Antarctic (Australia v Japan, New Zealand intervening)* [2013], ICJ Pleadings 1, 23–48.

110 Mr. Johnson failed to mention: Press Release, British High Commission, Mauritius, 23 February 2017.

110 the pressure Britain was about to place: Kate McQue and Mark Townsend, "Windrush Scandal Continues as Chagos Islanders Are Pressed to 'Go Back,'" *Guardian* (28 July 2019) <https://www.theguardian.com/world/2019/jul/28/windrush-scandal-continues-in-crawley-as-chagos-islanders-told-go-back> accessed 17 November 2021.

111 In March the British government announced: Press Release, British High Commission, Mauritius, 31 March 2017.

111 They were supported by: Email, 25 May 2017 (on file with author).

112 Reports came in: Email, 1 June 2017 (on file with author).

113 the Congo . . . circulated a draft: UNGA Request for an advisory opinion of the ICJ on the legal consequences of the separation of the Chagos Archipelago from Mauritius in 1965 (A/71/L.73) (15 June 2017).

114 "The holding of the exhibit": Photograph, June 2017 (on file with author).

114 Britain warned that the General Assembly: "United Kingdom Note Verbale No. 357/2017."

115 "the part-Kenyan president's": Sewell Chan, "Boris Johnson's Essay on Obama and Churchill Touches Nerve Online," *New York Times* (22 April 2016) <https://www.nytimes.com/2016/04/23/world/europe/boris-johnson-the-sun-brexit.html> accessed 17 November 2021; Anushka Ashtana and Ben Quinn, "London Mayor Under Fire for Remark About 'part-Kenyan' Barack Obama," *Guardian* <https://www.theguardian.com/politics/2016/apr/22/boris-johnson barack-obama-kenyan-eu-referendum> accessed 17 November 2021.

PART FIVE: 2019

119 On the morning of 22 June 2017: "General Assembly Adopts Resolution Seeking International Court's Advisory Opinion on Pre-Independence Separation of Chagos Archipelago from Mauritius (Press Release) (GA/11924, 22 Jun 2017)" <https://www.un.org/press/en/2017/ga11924.doc.htm> accessed 17 November 2021; the video of the session is available at *The General Assembly Adopts a Resolution Seeking the International Court's Advisory Opinion on Pre-Independence Separation of the Chagos Archipelago from Mauritius, at 88th Plenary of the Seventy-First Session (22 June 2017)* <https://www.unmultimedia.org /avlibrary/asset/1916/1916290/> accessed 17 November 2017.

119 He spoke soberly: *The General Assembly Adopts a Resolution Seeking the International Court's Advisory Opinion on Pre-Independence Separation of the Chagos Archipelago from Mauritius, at 88th Plenary of the Seventy-First Session (22 June 2017)*, 36:08.

123 the United States intervened: "EM, Gonzalo Gallegos, Senior Advisor, Western Hemisphere Affairs, US Mission to the UN, Monday November 13, 2017, 11:14 a.m."

123 by the fifth round: Syed Akbaruddin, *India vs UK: The Story of An Unprecedented Diplomatic Win* (Harper Collins India, 2021), p. 129; *Security Council, General Assembly, Elect Four Judges to International Court of Justice at 8092nd and 8093rd Meetings (9 November 2017)* <https://www.unmultimedia.org/avlibrary /asset/2034/2034719/> accessed 17 November 2021; *The Security Council, Meeting Twice Today Independently from but Concurrently with the General Assembly, Elected Four Candidates to the International Court of Justice for Nine-Year Terms, Beginning on 6 February 2018 (9 November 2017)* <https://www.unmultimedia.org /avlibrary/asset/2033/2033019/> accessed 17 November 2021.

123 Britain's permanent representative: Letter, 15 November 2017 (on file with author).

123 London proposed the use: Article 12 of the ICJ Statute establishes a mechanism whose purpose is to overcome a deadlock—after three voting rounds—in the ordinary election procedure of judges to the Court, but has never been used; Bardo Fassbender, "Article 12," Andreas Zimmermann, Christian Tomuschat and Karin Oellers-Frahm (eds), *The Statute of the International Court of Justice: A Commentary*, 3rd edn (Kindle, Oxford University Press, 2012), paras 1–5; Statute of the International Court of Justice (26 June 1945), 33 UNTS 993, Article 12; Statute of the Permanent Court of International Justice (League of Nations, 16 December 1920, as amended 1929), Article 12.

124 The idea collapsed: Akbaruddin, *India vs UK*, p. 140.

124 The loss of the British judge: UK Parliament, Foreign Affairs Committee, "Loss

of ICJ Judge Is a Failure of UK Diplomacy" <https://committees.parliament
.uk/committee/78/foreign-affairs-committee/news/103324/loss-of-icj-judge-is
-a-failure-of-uk-diplomacy/> accessed 17 November 2021; Owen Bowcott,
"No British Judge on World Court for First Time in Its 71-Year History,"
Guardian <https://www.theguardian.com/law/2017/nov/20/no-british-judge
-on-world-court-for-first-time-in-its-71-year-history> accessed 17 November
2021.

124 If losing one vote: "To lose one parent, Mr. Worthing, may be regarded as a
misfortune; to lose both looks like carelessness," Oscar Wilde, *The Importance
of Being Earnest* (Kindle, Dover Publications, 1990), 28.

130 a French friend who appears often: Alain Pellet, "The Role of the International
Lawyer in International Litigation (Ch.9)," Chanaka Wickremasinghe et al.
(eds), *The International Lawyer as Practitioner* (British Institute of International and Comparative Law, 2000), 147–49.

132 "one of the harshest and most cruel": Abdulqawi Ahmed Yusuf, "Foreword,"
in Elena Carpanelli and Tullio Scovazzi, *Legal and Political Aspects of Italian
Colonialism in Somalia* (Giappichelli, 2020); Email, Yusuf to author, 24 April
2021.

132 "No country wishes": *Pleadings (hearing CR 2018/20) Legal Consequences of the
Separation of the Chagos Archipelago from Mauritius in 1965* [2018], ICJ Pleadings 1, 71.

133 "It concerns real people": *Ibid.*, 75.

134 Mr. Buckland accepted: *Pleadings (hearing CR 2018/21) Legal Consequences of
the Separation of the Chagos Archipelago from Mauritius in 1965* [2018], ICJ
Pleadings 1, 61.

135 "Thousands of forcibly displaced people": ICJ, Verbatim Records, CR 2018/22,
p. 9, 4 September 2018 (Ms. De Wet).

136 And so it went: The oral statements are available at https://www.icj-cij.org/en
/case/169/oral-proceedings.

136 "Not a single State argued": ICJ, Verbatim Records, CR 2018/27, p. 30,
6 September 2018 (Ms. Negm).

137 In the Chagos case, a bare majority: 24 white, 7 Black, 6 Hispanic, 4 Asian,
2 Arabic.

138 The deliberation after the hearing: After the oral phase, the judges meet in
private for a preliminary exchange of views. The President will submit a
written list of issues which in his or her consideration should be addressed
in the final decision. The judges can make comments and suggest amend-
ments thereto. Thereafter, each judge prepares a note with tentative views
on how the case should be adjudicated. These notes are circulated to all the
bench. Deliberations take place after these initial steps with a view to shape
the overall substance of the eventual judgement. It is only after these deliberations that a drafting committee consisting of three judges (or more if the
Court so decides) is constituted. The drafting committee circulates a draft
confidential judgement in respect of which the rest of the bench can submit
comments. The draft is given a "first reading" in multiple private meetings:
each paragraph is discussed to decide whether to leave it as is or amend it. The
amended draft judgement goes through the same process prior to being given

a "second reading," after which a final vote is taken. That vote is incorporated into the operative section of the judgement. Judges may append separate or dissenting opinions. *Handbook of the International Court of Justice* (United Nations, 2016), 71–72 <https://legal.un.org/avl/pdf/rs/other_resources/man uel_en.pdf> accessed 17 November 2021.

144 The Court's ruling was widely reported: "Mauritius: UN Top Court Tells UK to End Rule of Chagos Islands 'Rapidly.'" *All Africa* (25 February 2019) <https://allafrica.com/stories/201902260553.html> accessed 17 November 2021; "UN Court Says Britain Should 'Rapidly' Give Up Chagos Islands," *Al Jazeera* (25 February 2019) <https://www.aljazeera.com/news/2019/2/25/ un-court-says-britain-should-rapidly-give-up-chagos-islands> accessed 17 November 2021; "UN: Britain Should 'Rapidly' Give Up Chagos Islands," *Voice of America* (25 February 2019) <https://www.voanews.com/a/un-britain -should-rapidly-give-up-chagos-islands/4803217.html> accessed 17 November 2021; Owen Bowcott, "UN Court Rejects UK's Claim of Sovereignty over Chagos Islands," *Guardian* (25 February 2019) <https://www.theguard ian.com/world/2019/feb/25/un-court-rejects-uk-claim-to-sovereignty-over -chagos-islands> accessed 17 November 2021; "Chagos Archipelago Dispute: ICJ Rules against UK, Advises Rapid Decolonisation of Mauritian Islands," *India TV News* (25 February 2019) <https://www.indiatvnews.com /news/world-chagos-archipelago-dispute-icj-rules-against-uk-advises-rapid -decolonisation-of-mauritian-islands-506303> accessed 17 November 2021; "U.K. Should Hand Over Chagos Islands to Mauritius: ICJ," *The Hindu* (25 February 2019) <https://www.thehindu.com/news/international/uk-should -hand-over-chagos-islands-to-mauritius-icj/article26367827.ece> accessed 18 November 2021; "UN Demands UK Withdrawing Colonial Administration from Chagos Archipelago," *Xinhua Net* (23 May 2019) <http://www.xinhuanet .com/english/2019-05/23/c_138081226.htm> accessed 18 November 2021; "Humiliation for Britain as UN Demands It Ends Rule of Chagos Islands in Six Months," *South China Morning Post* (23 May 2019) <https://www.scmp .com/news/world/europe/article/3011410/stinging-defeat-britain-un-demands -it-ends-rule-chagos-islands> accessed 18 November 2021; "'Historic Moment to Bring End to Colonialism': UN Court Says UK Illegally Occupied Chagos Islands," *Russia Today* (25 February 2019) <https://www.rt.com/news/452 400-icj-uk-chagos-decision/> accessed 18 November 2021; "World Court— Britain Must Return Indian Ocean Islands to Mauritius," *Reuters* (25 February 2019) <https://www.reuters.com/article/uk-britain-mauritius-worldcourt -idUKKCN1QE1WX> accessed 20 November 2021; "U.N. Court Tells Britain to End Control of Chagos Islands, Home to U.S. Air Base," *New York Times* (25 February 2019) <https://www.nytimes.com/2019/02/25/world/asia/britain -mauritius-chagos-islands.html> accessed 20 November 2021.

145 a junior minister told Parliament: "HL Deb 26 Feb 2019, Vol 796 (Hansard)" <https://hansard.parliament.uk/lords/2019-02-26/debates/1F356B7D-4220 -404C-A9F3-C44834DFC8F0/ChagosArchipelago> accessed 20 November 2021.

145 "The United Kingdom respects the ICJ": "British Indian Ocean Territory Statement Made by Sir Alan Duncan (30 April 2019) (Written Questions,

Answers and Statements, UK Parliament)" <https://questions-statements
.parliament.uk/written-statements/detail/2019-04-30/HCWS1528> accessed
20 November 2021.

145 The leader of the opposition: Owen Bowcott, "Corbyn Condemns May's
Defiance of Chagos Islands Ruling," *Guardian* (1 May 2019) <https://www
.theguardian.com/world/2019/may/01/corbyn-condemns-mays-defiance-of
-chagos-islands-ruling> accessed 20 November 2021.

147 Prime Minister Jugnauth was the third: *UNGA Debate 22 May 2019, Request
for an Advisory Opinion of the International Court of Justice on the Legal Consequences of the Separation of the Chagos Archipelago from Mauritius in 1965 (General Assembly: 83rd Plenary Meeting, 73rd Session)* from 38:40, especially at 56:00
<https://media.un.org/en/asset/k18/k186t870d0> accessed 20 November 2021
(Prime Minister Jugnauth, Mauritius).

148 The sound of power shifting: UNGA Res 73/295 (Advisory opinion of the
International Court of Justice on the legal consequences of the separation of
the Chagos Archipelago from Mauritius in 1965) (2019).

149 Britain is firmly committed: *UNGA Debate 22 May 2019, Request for an Advisory Opinion of the International Court of Justice on the Legal Consequences of the
Separation of the Chagos Archipelago from Mauritius in 1965 (General Assembly:
83rd Plenary Meeting, 73rd Session)*, 2:50:30'. (Permanent Representative Karen
Pierce, UK.)

EPILOGUE: *BLEU DE NÎMES*

154 "The United Kingdom has no doubt": Letter dated 28 September 2021 from
the Permanent Representative of the UK to the UN Secretary-General, UN
doc A/76/368, 1 October 2021.

156 Without a licence from Port Louis: https://www.sure.io; Mauritius, Information and Communication Technologies Act 2001, Part VI.

156 Sportsbet.io, a betting company: "Sportsbet.io Website" <https://sportsbet.io
/sports> accessed 21 November 2021.

156 The Pobjoy Mint: "Sea Creatures: Clown Triggerfish—2021 Unc. Coloured
Cupro Nickel Diamond Finish 50p Coin—BIOT" <https://www.pobjoy
.com/us/sea-creatures-clown-triggerfish-2021-unc-cupro-nickel-diamond
-finish-50p-coin-biot> accessed 21 November 2021.

157 The renowned Zoological Society of London: "UK Overseas Territory—
Chagos Archipelago (Zoological Society of London)" <https://www.zsl.org
/regions/uk-overseas-territories/chagos-archipelago> accessed 21 November
2021.

157 MRAG, a modest British company: "Scientific and Technical Advice for
the Management of Maritime Waters in British Indian Overseas Territory
(BIOT) (MRAG)" <https://mrag.co.uk/experience/scientific-and-technical
-advice-management-maritime-waters-british-indian-overseas> accessed 21 November 2021.

157 With increasing frequency and force: Human Rights Watch is currently preparing a report.

157 Yet there is support for the charge: Decision Pursuant to Article 15 of the Rome

Statute on the Authorisation of an Investigation into the Situation in the People's Republic of Bangladesh/Republic of the Union of Myanmar, ICC-01/19-27, 14 November 2019.

157 President Joe Biden's assertion: "Remarks by President Biden on America's Place in the World," The White House (4 February 2021) <https://www.whitehouse.gov/briefing-room/speeches-remarks/2021/02/04/remarks-by-president-biden-on-americas-place-in-the-world/>

157 with which to beat Russia: UN General Assembly resolution 68/262 ("Territorial Integrity of Ukraine"), 27 March 2014.

157 and China (for failing . . .): South China Seas Arbitration, Republic of Philippines v People's Republic of China, Award of 12 July 2016, <https://pcacases.com/web/sendAttach/2086>

158 An early step was to change its map: "United Nations Map Marks Chagos Islands as Mauritian Territory" (Chagossupport.org) <https://www.chagossupport.org.uk/post/2020/06/29/united-nations-map-marks-chagos-islands-as-mauritian-territory> accessed 20 November 2021.

158 The Food and Agriculture Organisation: Following its withdrawal from the EU, on 1 January 2021, the UN did not allow the UK to ratify the Agreement as a coastal state (documents on file with the author).

158 The Universal Postal Union: "UPU Adopts UN Resolution on Chagos Archipelago (Press Release) (25 Aug 2021)" (Universal Postal Union) <https://www.upu.int/en/Press-Release/2021/Press-release-UPU-adopts-UN-resolution-on-Chagos-Archipelago>; Alex Chaplin, "How a Territorial Dispute Made the Universal Postal Union Declare Stamps Illegal," 135, *American Philatelist* (2021), 1098–1105.

158 This is known as the *Monetary Gold* principle: *Monetary Gold Removed from Rome in 1943 (Italy v France, United Kingdom and United States of America)*, 1954, ICJ Reports 19.

158 ITLOS rejected the argument: *Dispute Concerning Delimitation of the Maritime Boundary Between Mauritius and Maldives in the Indian Ocean (Mauritius/Maldives) (Preliminary Objections)* [2021], ITLOS Rep 1 para 246.

159 "no effect" for Britain: "British Indian Ocean Territory Questions for Ministry of Defence (3 Feb 2021) (Written Questions, Answers and Statements, UK Parliament) (J Heappey)" <https://questions-statements.parliament.uk/written-questions/detail/2021-02-03/148829> accessed 20 November 2021.

POSTSCRIPT: SPRING 2023

167 In November 2022: Statement by Secretary of State for Foreign, Commonwealth and Development Affairs to UK Parliament, November 3, 2022, Statement UIN HCWS354; Statement by Prime Minister Pravind Jugnauth to National Assembly, November 3, 2022, *Hansard,* 19–20; Human Rights Watch, *"That's When the Nightmare Started": The UK and US Forced Displacement of the Chagossians and Ongoing Colonial Crimes,* February 15, 2023.

Further Reading

NON-FICTION

Robert Scott, *Limuria: The Lesser Dependencies of Mauritius* (Oxford University Press, 1961)

Richard Edis, *Peak of Limuria: The Story of Diego Garcia and the Chagos Archipelago* (Friends of the Chagos, 2004)

David Vine, *Island of Shame: The Secret History of the U.S. Military Base on Diego Garcia* (Princeton, 2009)

Sandra Evers, *Eviction from the Chagos Islands* (Brill, 2011)

Laura Jeffery, *Chagos Islanders in Mauritius and the UK: Forced Displacement and Onward Migration* (Manchester University Press, 2011)

Stephen Allen, *The Chagos Islanders and International Law* (Hart Publishing, 2014)

Nigel Wenban-Smith and Marina Carter, *Chagos: A History—Exploration, Exploitation, Expulsion* (Chagos Conservation Trust, 2015)

Nando Bodha, *L'Archipel du Chagrin* (Immedia, 2018)

Thomas Bürri and Jamie Trinidad, *The International Court of Justice and Decolonisation: New Directions from the Chagos Advisory Opinion* (Cambridge, 2021)

Florian Grosset, *The Chagos Betrayal: How Britain Robbed an Island and Made Its People Disappear* (Myriad Editions, 2021) (a graphic novel)

NOVELS

Shenaz Patel, *Silence of the Chagos* (Restless Books, 2019) (translated by Jeffery Zuckerman from the French, *Le Silence de Chagos*, 2018)

Caroline Laurent, *Rivage de la Colère* (Les Escales, 2020)

Natasha Soobramanien and Luke Williams, *Diego Garcia* (Fitzcarraldo Editions, 2022)

POETRY

Saradha Soobrayen, "Out of Place, Out of Language, Out of Home" (from *Crossings: Journal of Migration and Culture*, 2019)

THEATRE

Adrian Jackson, *A Few Man Fridays* (Oberon Books, 2012)

DOCUMENTARY

John Pilger, *Stealing a Nation* (2004)

Index

PICTURE CREDITS

A NOTE ON THE TYPE

This book was set in Adobe Garamond. Designed for the Adobe Corporation by Robert Slimbach, the fonts are based on types first cut by Claude Garamond (ca. 1480–1561). Garamond was a pupil of Geoffroy Tory and is believed to have followed the Venetian models, although he introduced a number of important differences, and it is to him that we owe the letters we now know as "old style." He gave to his letters a certain elegance and feeling of movement that won their creator an immediate reputation and the patronage of Francis I of France.

Composed by North Market Street Graphics,
Lancaster, Pennsylvania

Printed and bound by Berryville Graphics,
Berryville, Virginia

Designed by Cassandra J. Pappas